Quality Learning for Student Teachers:

University Tutors' Educational Practices

Edited
by
Della Fish

David Fulton Publishers
London

David Fulton Publishers Ltd
2 Barbon Close, London WC1N 3JX

First published in Great Britain by
David Fulton Publishers 1995

Note: The right of the authors to be identified as the author of this work
has been asserted by them in accordance with the Copyright, Designs and
Patents Act 1988.

Copyright © Della Fish, Robert Catt, Christine Edwards, Hilma Rask,
Tom Sweeny and Lynne Thorogood

British Library Cataloguing in Publication Data

A catalogue record for this book is available from the British Library

ISBN 1-85346-352-3

Typeset by Action Typesetting Limited, Gloucester

Printed in Great Britain by BPC Books & Journals, Exeter

Contents

Acknowledgements

I acknowledge with gratitude the help of the following people and organisations in the preparation of this publication. Research funds via West London Institute from the Higher Education Funding Council of England provided time for my colleagues for the writing up of the case studies and for some of the editorial work. Dr Michael Golby, Reader in Education, Exeter University offered very helpful comments on the penultimate draft and drew my attention to the work of Shirley Grundy and to the Michael Oakeshott essay. Jamie Davidson helped with the preparation of the final draft for Chapters 3, 4 and 5 and gave advice about word processing at vital moments. And Evelyn Usher proofread and corrected drafts with endless patience and good humour.

Special thanks to my colleagues who provided the case studies and only smiled and responded unfalteringly when I became fierce. They would wish to join with me in acknowledging and thanking for their willing co-operation the many students alongside whom we have learnt about teaching and teacher education, some of whom have been involved in the studies reported in Part 2.

Any errors, failures or omissions are mine alone. Any opinions expressed in the editor's chapters are entirely mine, do not necessarily reflect the views of my colleagues and are in no way associated with either the establishment that was called West London Institute and is now a part of Brunel University or with Exeter University.

Editor

List of Abbreviations

AT	Attainment Target
BA/BSc/QTS	Bachelor of Arts/Bachelor of Science with Qualified Teacher Status
CATE	Committee for the Accreditation of Teacher Education
CNAA	Council for National Academic Awards
DES	Department of Education and Science
DFE	Department for Education
GCSE	General Certificate of Secondary Education
GEST	Grants-related Educational Support for Teachers
HE	Higher Education
HEFCE	Higher Education Funding Council for England
HEI	Higher Education Institution
HMI	Her Majesty's Inspector
HMSO	Her Majesty's Stationery Office
ILEA	Inner London Education Authority
INSET	In-service Education and Training of Teachers
ITE	Initial Teacher Education
ITT	Initial Teacher Training
LEA	Local Education Authority
LMS	Local Management of Schools
MOTE	Modes of Teacher Education
NCC	National Curriculum Council
NDS	Normal Desirable State
NFER	National Foundation for Educational Research
OFSTED	Office for Standards in Education
PGCE	Postgraduate Certificate of Education
SCAA	Schools Curriculum and Assessment Authority
SRHE	Society for Research into Higher Education
TES	*Times Education Supplement*

| TP | Teaching Practice |
| TTA | Teacher Training Agency |

Special notes

The term 'Education Studies' denotes a component of teacher education courses, and should not be confused with more general references to 'education studies'.

For clarity, the works of David Carr and Wilfred Carr are referred to in the body of the text using either their Christian names or initials in addition to their surname, as appropriate, and not simply their surname, since their subject matter and publication dates are similar.

Notes on the Contributors

Robert Catt is a senior lecturer in Education at Brunel University, and teaches Educational Studies within a BA/BSc/QTS secondary course. Prior to his work in higher education he taught English in secondary schools, both in London and on the south coast, and was head of English and drama in a large comprehensive school. He has a particular interest in the speaking and listening curriculum and has contributed articles to journals of education.

Della Fish has worked in initial teacher education for twenty-five years. She currently works as a freelance consultant and offers a masters degree in the supervision and development of professional practice for mentors across the caring professions at Brunel University. Until recently she was a principal lecturer in Education and before that was a senior lecturer in English at Hereford College of Education. She has researched and published on the pre-service preparation of students not only in teacher education, but also across a wide range of other professions, and has worked in Poland with teacher trainers. She has recently been appointed honorary research fellow at the School of Education, Exeter University.

Christine Edwards studied at the Royal Academy of Music. She worked as a music specialist in a secondary school before becoming involved in primary music. After five years as a generalist classroom teacher she became a music support teacher for the London Borough of Hounslow. In 1989 she shared her advisory role with a role in West London Institute of Higher Education, working part time on the primary BEd and PGCE courses. She currently works for most of her time in higher education, but still provides INSET work for some London Boroughs.

Hilma Rask is currently a senior lecturer at Brunel University. Her previous teaching experience has taken place in a wide range of education settings from nursery through to adult education. She has had lengthy involvement in advisory work and in INSET. She has particular interests in international and comparative education, bilingualism and education in the earliest years.

Tom Sweeney is currently a senior lecturer in Education at Brunel University working on primary and secondary initial teacher education courses. He is course leader for the secondary BA/BSc/QTS course and regularly works in primary and secondary schools as a teacher of drama. Until 1986 he held a joint post as director of staff training at an Outer London comprehensive school and as a senior lecturer on initial courses at a college of higher education. He has experience as a local education authority advisory teacher and regularly runs in-service courses in drama. His publications include articles on the reform of teacher training and the teaching of drama and the arts. He also works in North America as visiting lecturer at Towson State University where he teaches on in-service programmes for primary and secondary teachers.

Lynne Thorogood was a primary school teacher for eleven years, including undertaking both deputy head and acting headship responsibilities. She has been a senior lecturer at West London Institute (now Brunel University) for seven years, teaching language education and art education and is course leader for the PGCE primary. Her publications include: 'Purpose and audience in children's writing' (October, 1984) *Child Education*; 'Fostering development in the writing of eight year olds' (with B. Raban) (1985) *Reading*, **19** (2), reprinted in Mercer, N. (Ed.) (1988) *Language and literacy from an educational perspective* Milton Keynes: Open University Press; and 'Drafting, revising and a matter of time' (December 1988) Links, **14** (1).

Foreword

How are teachers of the future to be educated? There can surely be no more important a question, for education carries the genetic codes for our collective social future. Yet, given the profundity of the question, the answers which we have lately offered to encumber our children and their children's children are astonishingly superficial. We have allowed the immediate and trivial preoccupations of the politics of the day, often matters of personality rather than principle, to drive out responsible deliberation in a properly longer-term perspective. Education in schools, colleges and universities has been a political football over the past twenty years or so. Most recently, teacher education has been the subject of radical restructuring threatening to take it away from academic attachments and traditions built up and struggled for over a hundred years and more.

Within these relatively recent debates and the headlong rush to legislate, the word 'quality' has been severely compromised. Who can dispute that 'quality' is what is needed in education, as elsewhere? But who but an ignoramus could announce by declaiming this mantra to have solved educational riddles disputed down the ages by minds and spirits every bit as exercised in their times as we in ours? It is noteworthy that this particular shibboleth is confronted in the very title of this book. Moreover, there runs through the whole book a discussion and demonstration of educational quality that will confront open-minded readers with their own prejudices.

This book contests the premature closure of educational questions that has characterised the recent past. Educational questions are open questions, as we in a pluralistic and democratic society have every reason to understand if we have eyes to see and ears to hear. Educational questions are open questions precisely because there exist legitimately different views about the 'good life' with no known means to arbitrate among them. Hence schools, colleges and universities are places where various ways of life and expectations for the future meet — and sometimes inevitably conflict. Teachers and the curriculum they teach are at the centre of such conflicts.

There is at present a false, and inevitably temporary, consensus about the curriculum. Does all that is worth knowing and necessary to know reside in ten or eleven school subjects (of all the hundreds of subjects scholars engage in)? Can the proficient transmission of currently approved versions of these subjects suffice as a foundation for young people whose children will be living at the end of the twenty-first century?

If school teachers do not understand the significance of these questions, there can be little hope of the general public doing so. These are not arm-chair theoretical questions. They take daily substance in teachers' everyday work with pupils and students. They will recur in our political culture long after, and probably before, the expiry of the five-year 'moratorium' on curriculum change proposed by Dearing and accepted by government in 1994. Thus we are dealing with momentous questions which take detailed practical form, and concern both the general public and the education profession alike.

This book takes all this seriously. Della Fish and her colleagues have provided us with a clear set of statements of the art of educating teachers. Here we are able to see and begin to understand what is going on when students are encouraged to review their practical teaching in its full complexity. The book is important because the teacher education community has neglected the task of making its work known to a larger public. Teacher educators have been too busy responding to external demands, often inimical to their deeper educational aims, to cultivate public approval. This book makes an important start on the processes not merely of gaining approval, but of generating public discussion, necessary to any proper and socially responsive development of teacher education.

From such a discussion could come several inestimable benefits. First, teacher education could become demythologised. There is no 'barmy theory' in these pages. Second, the climate of vilification that has afflicted the field for years could be dispelled — a necessary condition for better public confidence. Third, teacher educators themselves could proceed with less trepidation. This will be crucial in the next few years as tutors new to teacher education, especially from the schools, take up the challenge. The heritage of good practice here recorded, fragmentary as it must be — for it is an unfinished art — is one that our successors have the right to evaluate.

Our authors are far too realistic to imagine that all of this could come from a single publication considered alone. But it is a significant beginning in the presentation of evidence — let us hope that there will be more — attesting to the turning of a particularly dark and dangerous corner in our cultural history.

Michael Golby
Reader in Education
Exeter University School of Education
September 1994

Introduction

Broad aims

This book provides specific evidence about aspects of the educational practices of tutors who work in traditional forms of initial teacher education (ITE). It presents an illuminative view of some of the educational roles they fulfil and captures, for the record, processes central to their work. It challenges the unsupported and erroneous rumours spread by the media that higher education (HE) offers student teachers irrelevant theory, and that education tutors are agents of left-wing indoctrination. It offers for debate a view that the work currently carried out by the HE tutor plays a vital role in the professional preparation of teachers.

In making changes to the way teachers are to be prepared, the government has commissioned no research, made public no evidence and encouraged no debate about the contribution of education tutors from higher education institutions (HEIs). And HE has itself been slow to communicate to teachers in schools and the public at large the essential nature of a role whose scope is extremely broad. Recent legislation has now paved the way for a major reduction in or even the total cessation of education tutors' work in ITE, by moving the entire system away from school-based partnerships between schools and HE and towards a school-centred initial teacher training (ITT) scheme in which schools can operate alone. But the preparation of student teachers is not yet exclusive to schools alone, and the new teacher trainers, wherever they are based, will, as they design new courses and consider their various contributions to the new system, still need to take account of the work currently carried out by the HE tutor.

The thesis of the book is that *part* of the evidence of what such work currently comprises is to be found, via some specific examples of tutors' practices, in a principled understanding of some processes central to the tutor's role. In providing a small window on such processes, and by calling for the sharing of other evidence about the tutor's role (for example, of the scope of it and the depth of its educational content), it is hoped to influence those vital discussions about partnership between teacher-mentor and tutor in school-based schemes and to demonstrate the need for this work to be part of them. It might also offer considerable food for thought to teachers operating in school-centred schemes where there is no higher education dimension.

The context

The mid-1990s have been full of *rumour* about the government's projected radical reform of teacher education, and also much influenced by the anti-intellectual arguments for a new cost-effective, on-the-job training for the teaching profession. But it is actions by government that illuminate intentions and motives. For example, the White Paper, *The reform of teacher training* (HMSO 1993), stated a commitment on the part of government to a continued if developing role for HE in ITE. Yet at the same time it offered new proposals for extending school-centred ITT, and put out key circulars – *9/92* and *14/93* (DFE 1992 and DFE 1993, respectively) – that required the HE tutor to change from being an educator to becoming a controller of quality. Further, the White Paper's proposals were made without existing models of school partnership having been fully developed, extended or evaluated. And these major 'reforms' were produced without inviting genuine consultation from those with expert insiders' knowledge and without acknowledging or considering the many responses and representations made hitherto by teachers and tutors regarding the training proposals issued in previous months. It is hardly surprising then that in largely unaltered form they subsequently became an Education Act in late July 1994.

But legislation had already been pre-empted by other less visible moves. Long before this Act was passed, major changes were made to the initial training system by manipulation of resources. Education establishments were already required to transfer much of the fees they earned from student teachers into their partner schools to cover the cost of the increased work done by teachers. The Open University, encouraged by government to the tune of £2.4 million, had provided a distance-learning approach to learning to teach. At a stroke this extended access to the profession and offered a challenge to existing higher education providers. It began, in 1992, with 1,300 places for intending primary and subject-specific secondary teachers. By June 1994, the *Times Education Supplement* (*TES*) had revealed to teachers that 12,000, had joined the February 1994 eighteen-month PGCE secondary course and that the primary PGCE course, due to start in February 1995, was already full (Pyke 1994). Further, in 1993, 250 of the 1993/94 cohort of 60,000 teacher training students were trained in school-centred pilot projects, and by May 1994 John Patten had announced a further 450 places for this scheme.

Despite these moves, it is hard to believe that the schools (whose main function is to educate pupils) will be able, alone, to provide teacher training courses of a reliably high standard and quality. They are still burdened with implementing the National Curriculum, managing devolved budgets, and introducing appraisal schemes. Yet the required reforms are not only centred on those same schools, but are also currently sweeping away (in the name of economies rather than of improved education) the following:

- traditional three- and four-year teacher education courses

- school/college partnerships, before they have had time to flourish

- the improved work of tutors with students, developed during the last twenty years but not highlighted by tutors to the public at large

- traditional freedom of choice about the focus of education research (in future most of the money for research into teaching will be available only through the Teacher Training Agency (TTA)).

As part of the rhetoric designed to pave the way for these changes, education tutors have been at worst vilified and at best ignored. In their place may soon be put further distance-learning packs or one-hour-per-week school-based seminars run by hard-pressed teachers or one-off outside speakers. HE for the student teacher is thus in danger of being replaced totally by a cheaper but narrowed view of teaching based on an old and outdated vocational training model. Short-term economic gains are prevailing over long-term educational ones. Testimony to the character and quality of what may ultimately be lost is available in the central section of this book.

Intentions

Although the government has already imposed the frameworks for these changes, and teachers have been made the leading partners in preparing student teachers, the execution of these matters on the ground will still require the providing partners to discuss and negotiate their specific roles and contributions to the education of the students. This book seeks to fuel these discussions and debates by clarifying and illuminating some aspects of tutors' educational procedures and by investigating their present practice through case studies which are interrogated for the prevailing themes, skills and processes. It notes five main processes which are central to the tutors' work and attempts to develop a principled understanding of the most central of these. It argues that only by reference to this level of understanding will the partners be in a proper position to decide what aspects of these processes should be incorporated into the teacher's mentoring role, what to preserve in its current or a revised form, and what to develop for the future.

In offering this contribution, the writers of these studies see ITE not only as providing efficient class teachers but also as preparing students to work effectively as professionals and as sustaining them beyond their first year of professional practice. They believe that it distorts the holistic nature of education to think that one can offer a relatively simple training base in classroom skills first and to seek only later in the teacher's career to build upon that base a grasp of educational issues. Even from the beginning of working with pupils as a student teacher, the deployment of skills calls for an educated understanding of when, why and how to employ them, and this cannot be gained solely from specific practice situations. They therefore see the role of HE as providing students with the vital intellectual and affective challenge of engaging with the study of education, of understanding themselves as professional practitioners and of stimulating and responding to intellectual curiosity. Without this, they argue, teachers will not have been adequately prepared to take responsibility for the education of pupils, which Dearing has already demonstrated goes beyond delivering the National Curriculum and which involves the exercise of professional judgement and educational understanding (Dearing 1993, pp.20−2). The considerable expertise with which these tutors enable students to gain a wider understanding (by attending to the different voices of students, teachers, and educational thinkers and researchers) is illustrated in Part 2.

Audience

This book is addressed to teachers (both primary and secondary) who will become (or are already) mentors for the new school-based or school-centred system of ITE. Many teachers already involved in mentor training are asking for far more details than they have ever had before about:

- how current courses are organised and how their quality is assured

- what the HE dimensions of those courses really seek to achieve

- what is the tutor's contribution to preparing a student to be a teacher

- what skills, knowledge, strategies and processes their work involves

- how the students respond to this work.

This book attempts to offer one small and partial response to this. It also seeks to arouse the attention of, and to engage in adding to this work, tutors in HE whose educational contribution to ITE has rarely been analysed publicly, and whose own established reflective practices and quality assurance procedures are mainly unsung outside the colleges.

This work might also be of interest to the students themselves, to research students who are working in the area of teacher education and to the governors and parents who are increasingly involved in decision-making about ITE.

Organisation of the book

The book is divided into three parts. The first part offers two chapters which provide a framework for understanding the present role of HE in and the contribution of the tutor to ITE. The first chapter looks at how government has attempted to undervalue the educational aspects of HE in ITE and to turn the tutor into an agent of quality control. It also looks at the (largely unknown) changes that have been made to education studies in the last twenty years and at those philosophical models that currently shape teacher education provision and their quality assurance procedures. The second chapter in this section provides a basis for considering the case studies of Part 2 of the book. It explains the research approach taken by the writers of the case studies, provides the necessary background details to the studies presented in Part 2 and comments on how these cases were scrutinised and how they are treated in Part 3.

The five case studies offered in Part 2 are drawn from across the range of ITE. They show work in undergraduate four-year and postgraduate one-year courses, and consider work with students preparing for both the primary and secondary age-ranges. The cases focus round reflection on and deliberation about practical teaching and learning. They offer insights into collaboration between a range of adults in early years classrooms, an educational studies programme, music in a Creative Arts programme, views of classroom display, and work on a drama project. But in addition to giving a flavour of what happens in college classrooms, these case studies provide something of a view of the rich mixture of work carried out in the initial training part of an education department's work, and also provide insight into the skills, strategies and approaches of those who currently teach teachers.

The third part contains three chapters. As a result of a careful analysis of the case studies, the first of these chapters illustrates, and explores in relation to some theoretical perspectives, some of the intentions, expertise and activities that characterise the work of the tutors as they develop students' educational understanding. Some of their achievements are highlighted, a key issue for tutors generally is revealed via a critique of the studies, and some helpful theoretical perspectives are offered. The second chapter focusses on tutors' development in students of practical discourse, which is seen as a central thrust of their work, and attention is drawn to some conditions necessary for this vital activity. In the final chapter, some future ways forward are discussed for supporting, continuing and extending this work, and a final proposal is made.

Della Fish
September 1994

References

Dearing, R. (1993) *The National Curriculum and its assessment*. London: SCAA.

DFE (1992) *Initial teacher training (secondary phase) (Circular 9/92)*. London: DFE.

DFE (1993) *The initial training of primary school teachers: new criteria for courses (Circular 14/93)*. London: DFE.

HMSO (1993) *The government's proposals for the reform of initial teacher training*. London: HMSO.

Pyke, N. (1994) '12,000, minus two pushes OU to limit', *Times Educational Supplement* (3.6.94), p.12.

Part 1

Initial Teacher Education
and the Tutor's Role:
Contextualising the Tutor's Practice

CHAPTER 1

Perspectives on the Tutor's Role: Quality Education versus Quality Control

Introduction

This chapter seeks to provide a context for the following case studies by attempting to illuminate the present pressures upon and dilemmas surrounding the education tutor's role in ITE and by offering some interpretations of its recent history. In doing so, a range of perspectives is drawn upon. First, a reminder is offered of debates about the nature of a university and the role of HE in professional training. The growth of the notion of quality control is also described. Second, the philosophical bases and the language of present ITE courses are considered, together with concepts and views of quality embedded in the two models which influence current practice. Recent attempts to replace the tutor's educational contribution by an entirely administrative role in quality control are noted. Third, the historical context of the tutor's work is examined, government publications since 1981 are considered and the gradual (and arguably deliberate) erosion of the importance of education, and therefore of the tutor in ITE, are highlighted. The changes through which education studies have passed are traced through the last two decades, and an increasing divergence is revealed between the view of theory held by many teachers who were trained some years ago and the present role of theory on recent courses. Challenges to tutors' knowledge, and some responses to this from within HE, are shown inadvertently to have contributed to the demise of the tutor. Finally, some questions are raised for the partners to ask themselves as they negotiate the future shape of ITE.

4

(i)

HE and professional preparation

The speed of change, the demands of accountability and the inappropriate imposition of the principles of market economy to all sectors of public service in the last two decades of the twentieth century have caused profound questions to be asked of some of our most fundamental traditions, values, practices and even our long-established institutions. These include the questioning of the nature of HE, of the relationship between HE and professional training and of what should constitute professional preparation as a whole. To these questions have now been added anxieties about how to assure the public and the paymasters about the quality of education. As a result, we should perhaps remember that the debates between the partners in ITE about how to shape their contributions to the preparation of future teachers, are only one part of, and are related to, a much wider series of political changes being made.

Universities today

As Schnur and Golby point out, debates about the idea of a university go back at least to Cardinal Newman's principles of education set out in 'the idea of a university' in the 1850s (Schnur and Golby 1995, in press). Writing soon after the universities were assimilated into a system of HE as a result of the 1963 Report of the Committee on Higher Education, Oakeshott noted the substitution of socialisation for education, defining 'socialisation' as 'an apprenticeship to adult life – teaching, training, instructing, imparting knowledge, learning, etc. – governed by an extrinsic purpose' (Oakeshott 1972, p.39). He complained that:

> in times past English universities have often been indolent guardians of the engagement to educate and as often they have recovered, but for a generation now they have anticipated almost every design of governments to transform them into instruments of 'socialization'.
> (Oakeshott 1972, p. 44.)

Now, in the 1990s, the very nature of universities is being questioned, their traditional composition is being challenged and reshaped, their role in society is being narrowed and academic freedom itself appears to be under some threat. Indeed, in 1993, the British university sector was reshaped to include many new institutions. On the whole, however, these matters are not being publicly debated but rather changes are being quietly executed and made to seem inevitable by manipulation of resources. Nor is this a purely British issue. There are government pressures on HE here and abroad for the delivery of cost-effective training rather than independent pursuit of knowledge. Values have changed, and it is suddenly less attractive to governments to spend money on education, perhaps because they have become interested only in short-term benefits. (See, for example, Bullough and Gitlin 1994 and Griffiths and Tann 1992.) This has resulted in major changes to teaching and learning processes. Undergraduate numbers are being increased and courses are everywhere being pressed to reduce their educational aims and to transmit to their 'clients' – even, 'customers' – career-related knowledge rather than exploring ideas and practices. In the words of Christopher Frayling:

> Lecture theatres are preferred to workshops and studios, formal knowledge is valued over tacit and experiential knowledge, one-to-one tutorials automatically qualify for the heaviest of 'efficiency cuts'; and 'research' (in the sense and with the vocabulary, of university science departments) rather than iterative learning is the way to attract serious funding.
> (Frayling 1994, p.9)

This essentially instrumental view of what HE is about is apparently a result of the application to it of inappropriate and damaging notions from an industrial model of production, accountability and quality control. It is no wonder that the only way of imposing this on HE is via a system of inspection, control and financial penalties to which the adjective 'quality' is frequently applied like a scented aerosol to try to render it more acceptable.

The arguments, about whether, as an inevitable result of all this, academic freedom and autonomy have been reduced, give a flavour of current debates about university education (see, for example, the debates in the *Times Higher Educational Supplement* throughout May 1994). Bekhradnia, the director of policy at the Higher Education Funding Council for England (HEFCE), for example, argues that while academic autonomy in certain professional matters must remain (including the appointment of colleagues, selection of students and academic decisions and judgements), it is a matter 'entirely for the Government how much money it is willing to devote to higher education, how much for teaching and how much for research' since the State 'has a legitimate interest in the way its money is used'. He thus simplifies the debate by reifying the state and claiming that all that is in dispute are merely 'the boundaries of the State's legitimate interest and the legitimate province of the academics'. He also adds ominously:

> I quite see that worsening staff student ratios may in one sense be taken to restrict the freedom of academics – but there is no God-given right to any particular level of staff-student ratio – one has only to go to France, Germany, Italy or even the United States to see this.
> (Bekhradnia 1994, p.13)

The level of this argument seems to speak for itself, since committing one crime is hardly excused by the existence of another.

In contrast to this view, as Kelly has recently reminded us, is the notion that the 'prime responsibility of a university ... is not only to permit, but also to promote the process of continuous questioning – of challenge, critique, dialogue, debate, – which is the only route to the continued development of human knowledge and understanding' (Kelly 1993, p.128). He also reminds us that democracy itself is under threat:

> if society becomes incapable of seeing beyond the rhetoric with which governments of all colours dress up their policies, and has no means of mounting reasoned challenge to those policies, not least because lack of challenge removes the need for reasoned justification.

He adds:

> a university must be conceived as a politically independent centre for the fearless and impersonal pursuit of knowledge and understanding in all spheres, through a process of constant challenge to prevailing orthodoxies ...and, furthermore, ...the justification for the existence of this kind of centre is that it is a *sine qua non* of democratic living.
> (Kelly 1993, p.129)

Further, retaining a place for professional education inside HE is much more difficult when academic autonomy is eroded and politicians seem to be able to change its nature entirely, whenever they please. One temptingly easy solution to the difficulty of maintaining an educational role for HE against the pressures of job-oriented training is to bow to the pressures and remove from it those courses which seek to prepare students for a professional career, on the (inaccurate) grounds that skills training is not what universities should be offering. Thus there are motives for both government and university administrators and academics to argue for withdrawing the professional preparation of teachers from HE, but for neither party are the motives about improving education for the professions. By contrast, Schnur and Golby, writing about both the British and the American scenes, argue that universities must continue to offer ITE, since 'professionals in the field are always more conservative' than their counterparts in universities and that professional education must 'present a vision of the future as well as one for coping with the present' and equip professionals for a critical and innovative approach to their role (Schnur and Golby 1995, in press). Similarly, in Australia, Nance and Fawns argue, in contrast to their government's mechanistic ideas of quality in teaching, that:

> a systematic improvement in the quality and standing of teaching requires not only closer collaboration with schools, but also greater acceptance amongst academic staff that the university must assume greater public responsibility for the integrity of teacher education, its curriculum coherence, intellectual rigour and humanistic strength.
> (Nance and Fawns 1993, p.172)

HE and professional training

Interestingly, different professions have different relationships with the university sector. For example, the nursing profession (encouraged by the government) has recently moved its pre-service professional preparation into the university sector, and much money is being found for major new buildings in a number of universities for physiotherapy and occupational therapy departments (though often at a distance from all other buildings, and sometimes at least temporarily in hospitals off campus), while at the same time teacher preparation is being moved entirely out of the HE sector into on-the-job training in schools. Schnur and Golby make the interesting parallel point that both law and medicine have virtual autonomy and 'are often able to survive if not flourish in an environment of relative isolation within a university campus setting' (Schnur and Golby 1995, in press). In all cases these moves have apparently been made as a result of drawing unwarranted distinctions between learning how to practise and learning about practising. Again, Kelly makes the point that:

> teachers cannot be prepared to fulfil adequately their role in a democratic society without being required to engage in a properly

intellectual study of the activity they are engaged in, since it is not possible to practise that activity effectively without learning at the same time to reflect critically on that practice.
(Kelly 1993, p.130)

Here we have a glimpse of the educational role of the tutor. But at the moment there is an attempt to negate totally the tutor's current *educational* contribution and replace it with a *quality control* role, as part of moving teacher preparation entirely into the schools. This role has been made to seem to be a logical extension of the (industrially based) notion that both HE itself and professional training must be made to give evidence of its quality procedures. It would seem that the success of the government's arguments for this depends on public apathy about the importance of HE, ignorance about the present educational practices of tutors, lack of knowledge about quality control procedures, and acceptance of a deliberate attempt to nullify the tutor's role.

Quality control, HE and professional education

Until the 1980s quality control in HE was self-regulatory within universities, being maintained at the level of departments, and was externally provided by the Council for National Academic Awards (CNAA) for the non-university sector. The system was an elite one, and although it was not perfect it was helped to work by ease of resources and good staff/student ratios. This model became 'disturbed' when institutions began to be in direct competition with each other because of a mass system of HE which has made resources scarcer and introduced market forces (see Williams 1990, pp.72–3). A mass system means greater diversity of students' aims and of staff expertise. Clearly, the assurance of quality in a system like this is much more difficult than for an elite one. Whether that automatically means that we should have turned to the kind of approach to quality endemic in the manufacturing industry rather than to professionalism, however, is less clear. But that is what has happened.

In the 1990s, quality assurance for academic work in HE has been linked to funding via the HE funding councils for each country of Britain. As Taylor points out:

most institutions take their approach to quality from the 1989 White Paper on Higher Education, which defines **quality control** as the in-house means for maintaining and enhancing quality; **quality audit** as

the external mechanism for ensuring that suitable means of quality control are in place and working; and **quality assessment** as the process of externally reviewing and making judgements on teaching and learning in institutions.
(Taylor 1994, p.166)

As a result of the new requirements, most HEIs have set up committees and boards – and given staff special roles – in pursuit of quality control. Quality assurance procedures are also in place for teacher education via a requirement under the 1988 Education Reform Act, as well as under requirements of the Committee for the Accreditation of Teacher Education (CATE), the TTA and various education circulars. All of this will impact extensively upon partnership schools for ITE (see Fish 1995). The procedures required by this elaborate machinery, with its systems that are designed to double-check each other, are extensively time-consuming and seem in danger of becoming an end in themselves. As anyone who has ever devised rules knows, they are inclined to proliferate.

Thus (because professional as well as academic matters have to be protected) there are currently six systems of quality assurance which affect the preparation of teachers in HE, each demanding their own versions of quality review procedures and extensive resources. (In the face of this it is hardly surprising that many university administrators prefer to have places for 'straight subject' students as opposed to those on professional courses.) The six systems are as follows.

1. The external assessment procedures run by the HEFCE and HEFC for Wales (HEFCW). These 'ensure' the quality of teaching and learning in HE (and include self-assessment exercises which require extensive documentation and academic staff time).

2. Accreditation procedures set up by government and related to professional courses – first through two versions of CATE and now through the TTA. Accreditation means the careful scrutiny on behalf of government of the course proposals and procedures for teacher education courses and, more recently, the accreditation of *institutions* to offer courses. The very complexity of this machinery suggests a climate of suspicion of professionals.

3. Inspections on behalf of the Department for Education (DFE), run by the Office for Standards in Education (OFSTED),

stemming from and related to the professional side of the system. Inspections of ITE courses involve inspectors visiting schools so that they inspect the training elements in the school. In 1993/4 this involved some secondary schools in no less than *six* OFSTED visits in one academic year because their own inspection – when students were emphatically not required to be seen – was supplemented by five other inspections as the five HE providers who contributed students to the school were each also inspected. The TTA will no doubt perpetuate this system for the foreseeable future by subcontracting inspection of courses to OFSTED.

4. Extensive validation and review procedures set up within HE under senate via the course-running section of the university. Here new courses are scrutinised for academic standards, professional commitments as required by CATE and the TTA, and resource implications. These go through a number of committees before being recommended to senate. Existing courses are reviewed quinquennially (or more frequently for ITE since the government is always changing the requirements and demanding courses to be rewritten usually long before the five years are up).

5. In addition to this there are the annual quality control procedures at course and course subsection (module) level. These include internal arrangements to evaluate every individual module in writing, by students and staff, and course-by-course scrutiny of input, through-put and output figures (note the industrial language) as well as external academic moderation by the external examiner system.

6. Staff appraisal is also part of quality assurance. It is 'a process of assessing an individual's performance over a period of time against defined criteria of acceptable performance' (Loder 1990, p.43). This, as Loder goes on to say, implies that two things can be achieved: performance criteria can be clearly stated for any given post; individual staff performance can be measured against this. She also points out the tension between viewing appraisal as a means of improving performance and as a method of judging performance. Appraisal schemes rarely highlight weaknesses not already well-known and, having highlighted some issues, do nothing to change them. As Moses says, appraisal involves:

> a great deal of work for those academics who, having been chosen for senior positions by dint of their academic work are already

almost prevented from pursuing that work by the flood of paperwork, the endless committee meetings and the like...
(Moses 1989, p.104)

It seems more than odd that while industry in the mid-1990s is turning back to individual responsibility for quality, academics are increasingly treated as untrustworthy and unable to oversee their own. And this is why the kind of evidence that they can and do – as evinced by the studies in this book – is important.

If these issues are characteristic of HE in general and therefore contextualise the professional preparation of teachers, what can be said about ITE itself?

(ii)

ITE today

ITE today is dominated by two differing views of what is involved in being a teacher: the competency-based approach to ITE arising from a view that teaching is a matter of mastering techniques, skills, procedures; and the reflective practitioner philosophy of teacher education based on a notion that teaching essentially involves professional artistry. Most current ITE courses were designed on the basis of the reflective practitioner philosophy. (See the Modes of Teacher Education (MOTE) Research Project survey of ITE (Barrett *et al*. 1992).) The government has espoused the technical-ational model, apparently simply because it is cheaper and, being performance-based, yields more easily to industrial notions of quality control. In an attempt to standardise courses the government has now required (without any debate) all courses to take as their goals (aims) a set of prescribed competences (one list for all secondary students, and a slightly different list for all primary students). Most courses, unwilling to give up entirely their thought-through philosophy of how to prepare intending teachers, have retained as much as possible of their reflective practitioner approach and grafted on to this the required competences (see Fish 1995).

Current models of teacher education

Basically then, competency-based teacher education treats teaching as if it were an occupation rather than a profession. What matters most in training for this job is mastering specific and standardised skills and demonstrating that mastery. The skills are thus turned into competences and used as the means of assessing professional practice. This rather glib explanation hides a series of problems and difficulties — not least that dividing teaching into a series of skills is neither easy nor will the divisions be universally agreed. It is possible to argue that the thrust to accept and focus on competences in ITE comes from their apparent usefulness in ensuring quality, because they seem to offer simple measures of efficiency. This 'advantage' is more apparent than real, however.

The arguments for taking a reflective practitioner approach to ITE, derived from the professional artistry view of teaching, are as follows. The world of professional practice is fast changing. Professionals need to exercise and to continue to refine and develop not only simple skills, but their own dispositions, personality, professionalism, abilities, capacities and understandings. Many aspects of teaching a lesson cannot be pre-specified. Professionals need to be able to think on their feet, to improvise, to respond to the uncharted and unpredictable. Further, teaching is a moral and social practice requiring the ability to exercise moral decision-making and professional judgement. What is needed is an approach to teaching and to learning to teach which enables teachers 'to work at their practice, modify it and keep it under critical control' (Eraut 1989, p.175). It is generally agreed that reflective practice includes the following set of characteristics:

● taking practice *and* personal and formal theory seriously and being aware of their complexities

● taking a holistic view of professional practice

● taking a problem-solving stance to practice

● recognising the need for the practitioner to investigate practice personally and valuing small-scale humanistic enquiry as a means to this

● seeking the 'meaning in the experience' by means of reflecting on it

● seeking to identify beneath practice the values, assumptions, beliefs and personal theories (or 'theories of action')

● working in collaboration with colleagues, the better to reflect, deliberate and understand practise

● doing all of this in order to develop/change/refine/challenge practice.

Reflection, then, is one means of investigating practice and of theorising about it. Basically it involves systematic critical and creative thinking about action with the intention of understanding its roots and processes and thus being in a position to refine, improve or change future actions. Reflection touches matters that are both more intimate and more difficult to acknowledge than those considered by other approaches to investigating practice. Arguably also, it unearths issues that are at the very centre of understanding and refining practice.

Many who subscribe to the reflective practitioner approach argue that skills are important but that these are often context specific and can only be learnt *in situ*. They would argue that learning skills is useless without an educated understanding of how and when to use them and of the moral implications of the choices made. They would hold that the role of the educator of student teachers is to offer those elements, of the kind listed above, none of which can be simply picked up *in situ* (see Fish 1995).

Reflective practice is, of course, a concept that some teacher educators reject (see Gilroy 1993; Stones 1992). Others, however, like Kelly argue that it is: 'the only view which can reconcile the theory and practice of education ... [and is] the only justification for training teachers in a university setting' (Kelly 1993, p.132). Schnur and Golby see it as 'a slippery concept, full of promises yet to be redeemed', but consider that it offers 'the best chance of rescuing theory from political slaughter' (Schnur and Golby 1995, in press).

The underlying philosophies

A technical-rational view of professionalism lies under the competency-based approach to teacher education, and a professional artistry view of professionalism underlies the reflective practice approach to teaching.

Those subscribing to the technical-rational view see the preparation for teaching as offering would-be professionals a set of clear-cut routines and behaviours and a prepackaged content which requires only an efficient means of delivery. This cuts down considerably, they argue, the risks that professionals might fail to provide an *efficient*

14

service. It offers a series of certainties. This in turn makes assumptions that teaching and learning are relatively simple interactions in which the teacher gives out and pupils take in. Those subscribing to the professional artistry view, however, feel that the technical-ational view denies the real character of both professionalism on the one hand and teaching and learning on the other. They argue that teaching involves complex decision-making, and elements of professional judgement and practical wisdom, guided by moral principles, but that these are not able to be set down in absolute routines. They argue that recognising uncertainty is a better basis for learning to teach and that a professional, educated about the complexities of these decisions, is able to become an *effective* teacher — which is very different from being an efficient deliverer.

The technical-rational view characterises professional activities as essentially simple, describable and able to be broken down into their component parts (skills) and thus mastered. It regards being a professional as being essentially efficient in skills and submissive in harnessing them to carry out other people's decisions. This means 'the job of the teacher is re-defined along the lines of a technician' (Kydd and Weir 1993, p.409).

Opposed to this is the reflective practice view that behaving professionally is concerned with both means and ends. Here, the end is that of liberal education, professional activity is more akin to artistry, and practitioners are broadly autonomous, making their own decisions about their actions and the moral bases of those actions. Here the ability to exercise professional judgement (which is not a simple 'skill') is seen as essential. This view of professional practice considers that professional activity consists of components which cannot be entirely disentangled and treated separately. It takes a more holistic view.

Two notions of quality

Each model gives rise to a particular view of quality. The technical-rational model speaks in the language of quality control. It places emphasis upon visible performance within the practical aspects of the course. It seeks to test and measure these, believing that technical expertise is all-important and that learning cashes out immediately into visible products. Thus the model is behaviourist, emphasises fixed standards, controls the course via inspection and appraisal, believes that change can be imposed from outside the profession and that quality is measurable. It wishes to hold the professional practitioner accountable only for his/her technical expertise in achieving other people's goals. It is this approach to quality that the government has adopted and that is endemic in all the quality control procedures used in HE and ITE. It encourages the morally bankrupt notion that 'fitness for purpose' is a sufficient and appropriate aim for institutions of HE.

By contrast, the professional artistry view sees that there is more to professional practice than its surface and visible features. It believes that there is more to the whole than the sum of the parts, it believes in professional judgement, and holds that the most easily measurable is often also the most trivial. Further, it wishes to harness investigation, reflection and deliberation in order to enable professionals to develop their own insights from inside and views this as a better means of staff development than innovation imposed from without. In short, it believes that quality comes from deepening insight into one's own values, priorities, actions. Under this model it is possible to talk about wide professional answerability rather than narrow technical accountability, and the professional is in fact accountable for far more under this view than under the other. This introduces not only a responsibility for the moral dimensions of professional action, but also the responsibility to reflect upon, investigate and refine one's own practice. Here the evidence for quality would be found not in snap-shot observations and interviews, but in the documents that reveal the practitioner's preparation for and changes to practice, developing insights about teaching and learning, and investigations of his/her own practices, as well as in witnessing the *developing* practice itself. Much of this could be achieved in a professional development system.

Quality control and the role of the tutor

In both key government circulars which set out the requirements for ITE in England and Wales in the 1990s – *Circular 9/92* (DFE 1992) for the secondary sector, and *Circular 14/93* (DFE 1993) for the primary sector – one of the main roles for the HE tutor (indeed, the only specified role) is to administer the validation and accreditation procedures and to operate the system of quality control across schools who are partners in school-based schemes. It is not clear how this system was expected to operate, but some HEIs interpret it as checking-up on or overseeing the work of teachers and students in school by means of tutors making inspection-oriented, rather than education-oriented, visits. It is indeed ironic that tutors are seen only in administrative and quality control terms while teachers take over the whole educational role of working with students. The next section of this chapter seeks to consider how this state of affairs came to pass.

(iii)

History and fiction in ITE

This section looks at how government has managed to render redundant both theory and the role of the tutor, and at how Education Studies as a component of teacher education courses, in spite of being reconstituted, has been allowed to be both mis-understood and misrepresented.

The tutor rendered invisible

It would seem that the last two decades of the twentieth century have seen a systematic attempt by government to reduce the role of the tutor in ITE and ultimately to replace tutor with teacher. Indeed, as we have seen above, the government now requires an unequal partnership in ITE between schools and HEIs with teachers taking the lead. The idea of placing ITE entirely in the hands of teachers has been contrived to emerge during the 1980s and 1990s as a result of careful government orchestration and for reasons far from educational. (For a history of the swings between school and college, theory and practice, teacher and tutor across the nineteenth and twentieth centuries see Gardner (1993) and Fish (1989 and 1995).)

The broad developments since the 1980s have been from a *voluntary* involvement of teacher trainers in schools, as part of an individual institution's course development (led by the HEI), to an absolute requirement of full but teacher-led partnership as part of a fixed initial training curriculum, and ultimately to the notion that tutors are not required at all in school-centred teacher training. These changes have been managed by a series of government circulars and accompanying changes in resourcing which all those engaged in the ITE enterprise need to know about. (For fuller detail of the moves described below see Fish (1995).)

The period from 1981 to 1986 is the first of two phases in a strategy to nullify the role of HE in the preparation of teachers. The second phase, from 1988 to 1994, sees this strategy as far more overt and increasingly determined. The two periods together provide an historical context for looking at tutors' present practices.

The period 1981 to 1986 saw the publication of three discussion papers published by Her Majesty's Inspectors (HMI) (each one becoming less discursive and more prescriptive), a White Paper on teaching quality generally (designed to refocus the management of the teaching profession) and two DES circulars (designed to spell out the implications of government policy). All these make detailed reference to school/college partnership in ITE. Their tone and content at the time seemed, if increasingly irascible, at least at the start to be the result of genuine concern to improve ITE. But the documents were all assumption and assertion, and HE was slow to recognise that these were not papers designed to foster debate and improvement but to pave the way for a new training system (probably already fully conceived by government in the early 1980s and designed to save money).

In order to argue for *training* for future teachers rather than for the more expensive *education*, some of the extant aspects of ITE had to be demolished. By 1983, then, with *Teaching in schools: the content of initial training* (DES 1983a), skills were announced as the central and major content of teacher training, and theory was assumed to precede and barely to relate to practice. Within three months of this the government White Paper, *Teaching quality* (DES 1983b), was published. Under the guise of calling for improved quality in teaching, the Secretary of State for Education thus organised the machinery for taking control of teacher training and established CATE. By means of this he was to grant approval (accreditation) for courses − only when they conformed to his requirements. Power had passed to the politicians.

Fifteen months after *Teaching quality*, the first of many controlling government circulars, *Circular 3/84* (DES 1984), appeared. It began the task of increasingly narrowing down, simplifying and (as many would argue) distorting the task of ITT. Together with explicatory 'Catenotes' from the newly established CATE, this circular took control of the detail of initial training, reinforced the White Paper's comments and set up, via seventeen criteria which courses had to fulfil, a series of hurdles to be cleared by all institutions seeking to offer teacher training. Four of these seventeen criteria were about having links with and close working partnerships with schools, the use of experienced teachers in college and for assessment of students in school practice, recent and relevant experience for tutors, and substantial parts of the course to be based

in schools. The phrase 'adequate mastery of basic skills' appears
also. Wilkin notes that the Circular does not specify the role responsibilities, but the notion of 'recent and relevant' certainly suggests
that teachers and tutors are the same really and that neither party
has 'specific or remarkable skills'. As she observes:

> by extension, teacher training could be located in the schools with
> little depletion of quality since the college or department tutor has
> little that is unique to contribute. While the teacher must be retained,
> the tutor becomes marginalised if not dispensable. In this way it is
> suggested Circular 3/84 presaged the direction of future government
> policy on teacher training.
> (Wilkin 1990, p.14)

All this was further reinforced in 1986 by *Catenote 4, Links
between Initial training institutions and schools*. It looked to a
'common spirit of partnership through which both trainers and
teachers can make their own contributions towards a shared *professional* objective' [italics mine], (CATE 1986, p.7). What it did
not do, of course, was to provide extra resources to help the development of these partnerships. As a result, its actual effect was to
demand changes which it never permitted to become deep-rooted
and which could shortly be held up as not being implemented. This
then provided the basis for an even more dictatorial phase.

By 1988, then, a new approach to teaching and teacher training was
discernible. New routes to teaching were being devised to undercut
the power of the training institutions. Examples included the first
licensed teachers' scheme, heralded by *Qualified teacher status: a
consultation document* (DES 1988) and introduced by *Circular 18/89*.
It explicitly cut out the contribution of HE, unless the employer
chose to make the licensee attend an HE course. The whole approach
and language of the document and the arrangements come from
the world of business. It is about cost effective apprenticeship.

These moves, clearly aimed at breaking the power of HE over
teacher education, were closely followed by the publication of *Circular 23/89* (DES 1989) and its associated Catenote. This circular
transferred control over the ITE curriculum and content from the
colleges to the political arena, and gave the upper hand and the
maximum exposure to teachers. Tutors were barely mentioned, and
when they were it was in derogatory terms. Teachers were now to
be involved in planning courses and in their evaluation. The language of control and inspection had arrived. It is this move which
has further been crystallised by the two most recent circulars, *9/92*
(DFE 1992) and *14/93* (DFE 1993).

By the mid-1990s, then, a national ITT curriculum had been established, the universities had begun to withdraw from the fray, and teacher preparation had begun to be moved entirely into the schools. We are left with the question: what have education tutors actually been doing while all this rhetoric has been spilt in the political arena, and why have they not more ably defended their role?

Education studies caricatured

In 1989 it was commonly accepted in HEIs that there was still 'a deep-seated and very considerable reaction against the whole idea of theory' and that it was wrongly associated in the minds of practitioners with the study of what were called the foundation disciplines of education. It was also recognised that with the greater involvement of schools in ITE there was 'an enormous need for much groundwork to be done' in making 'all those involved in professional training . . . aware of the whole range of possible meanings of and approaches to theory' (Fish 1989, pp.58–9). By the mid-1990s the myths still persist.

The current caricature, encouraged by various Secretaries of State for Education, consists of the following ideas. Theory is useless and irrelevant to practice. It does not properly relate to practice. It should offer prescriptions that practitioners can immediately apply to practice. It either fails to offer them, or those it does offer do not work when applied in the classroom. Theory is something which education tutors foist upon and deliver to students in a setting away from practice and in isolation from it. These tutors have themselves lost touch with teaching. Thus, theory is flawed because it fails to offer practitioners useful prescriptions, and tutors are useless because they don't know anything about practice.

In fact theory is central to and underlies all practice, and to deny this is to demonstrate considerable ignorance of how practice operates. There are various perspectives on practice including personal theory (the values, beliefs, assumptions that lie beneath everything that sane people do) and formal theory (those *theories* or ideas offered by others and emanating from studies of matters related to practical education). Education Studies offered by tutors are not about 'how to do something' (which would be technical training) but, being a proper part of HE, are critical studies of practice and theory, exploring various ways of seeing and doing and the moral aspects of decision-making in the classroom and school. Here the activities are exploration, analysis, interpretation, appreciation (in its critical sense, from the arts). Tutors are teachers in their own right and their teaching *processes* are like those of teachers in schools in that they utilise a range of methods to enable their students to learn, though the level and direction of their work is different from that of their colleagues in school. They often draw attention to these in critical ways as part of their work with students. They also investigate their practice and seek to improve and refine it in ways they also recommend to their students. They (we!) are, however, culpable of having communicated few of these things to school partners and apparently none to the public at large. But examples of their work are offered in Sections 2 and 3 of this book.

How, then, have these two radically different views come to exist? One way of understanding this seems to be by looking at the trends in that aspect of teacher education known as Education Studies over the last three decades, during which, of course, many colleagues in school were trained. It is possible that they each experienced one example of the following but have assumed their experience to be typical and generalisable. And the fact that the many changes in the field have not been fully explained to those who work with students in school is certainly a failure to communicate on the part of tutors and HE.

Following Kelly, it is possible to discern three unfortunate trends in Education Studies: the foundation studies approach, the curriculum subjects approach and the practical skills approach. I shall then point to the Curriculum Studies approach as an example of a proper HE approach to professional education.

The first of the these trends seems to have left an indelible mark on the memories of teachers. It was an attempt, at its height in the late 1960s and early 1970s, to establish the academic credibility of Education as a subject, by offering new degrees in teacher education and, as Kelly says, 'injecting into [Education] a spurious form of academicism' (Kelly 1993, p.132). This was attempted by claiming that the foundation, or contributory disciplines of education, were the four so-called ugly sisters of history, sociology, psychology and philosophy. These new subjects which had 'of education' added to parent subjects to create their official name were indeed remote from practical matters, and certainly offered nothing towards a coherent theoretical underpinning for teaching. It proved to be what Schnur and Golby call a 'false dawn' for ITE (Schnur and Golby 1995, in press). Worse, it is this approach – now defunct for nearly twenty years – that has inevitably, gained theory a bad name. But then many changes have been made to school teaching too in the last twenty years, and teachers do not expect today to be castigated for methods and approaches that they stopped using two decades ago.

Following the demise of foundation studies came a move to try to pretend that all that was needed in terms of theory could be taught via the school curriculum (or school subject base). This is what Stones (1992) calls the fallacy that subject expertise, rather than teacher education, makes for good teachers. Although it is *possible* to come at the deeper matters of educational under-standing through a subject, it has often unfortunately proved to be more tempting simply to deal under this heading with matters to do with the 'delivery' of the subject and not to reach to the problematic and complex roots of the moral decision-making that underlie the teaching of subjects. This utilitarian view of Education Studies (the presentation to students of how to deliver, with no accompanying critical study of educational theory and practice) was encouraged by government in the CATE requirements of two years of subject study and the study of what they called the *application* of subjects.

The third unfortunate approach to Education Studies, namely the practical skills approach, has been encouraged by government some might say with a view ultimately to proving that since teachers can do this better in schools there is no need at all for student teachers to receive education in a university. The evidence of the government attempting to seduce university education to take up offering simple skills-based courses is to be found throughout the Catenotes which have accompanied every new government circular on ITE. One of the results of this has been the recruitment to education departments in HE of young teachers whose qualifications have emphasised their recent successful experience in the school classroom rather than given sound evidence of their ability to work at the level of principle and to analyse the theoretical underpinnings of their practice and contribute towards the development of spoken or written dialectic about practice. Worse, having appointed staff of this kind, education departments have not always offered the staff development that would have enabled new tutors to become experts in the study of education – mainly because they were too busy jumping to the latest twitch of the government's whip as expressed in the next Catenote.

The extent to which the government has been successful in requiring HE to contribute to its own downfall by adopting the skills-based approach is now borne out by a swing in the discussions in the professional ITE journals away from critique and towards questions about how to implement the competences. This is accompanied in some parts of HE by the sharp discouragement of staff from expressing views critical of government policy. But, as this text shows, tutors do exist who operate with students both powerfully and educationally (which to some extent must involve a critical perspective). And they do so mostly by adopting a Curriculum Studies approach.

Curriculum Studies is not about school timetables and subjects in a narrow sense. It is a field of study at postgraduate level which acknowledges the primacy of practice and seeks to bring to the deep exploration of practice all the analytical and interpretative scholarship of a wide range of formal theory. It rejects the boundaries between 'foundation disciplines' in education, the limitation of educational theory to the four disciplines of philosophy, sociology, psychology and history, and the division between theory and practice. It seeks to involve practitioners in research and scholarship across any range of practical and theoretical endeavours that might enlighten their work and improve their practice. It embraces the problematic rather than seeking simple instrumental solutions to practical problems. It recognises the complex relationship of theory and practice. It sees the practice of teaching as being related to traditions with recognised intentions that are moral and social, having as its end the promotion of knowledge for the public good. Its focus is *professional practice*, professional development, and the language and styles that are endemic to them. As such, it values both formal and personal theory which are practice-oriented. In short, Curriculum Studies as a field of endeavour supports the understanding of educational matters drawn from moral and critical perspectives that teachers need as a basis for their practical decision-making. Since its aims are to enable teachers to become thoughtful professionals, its perspectives are arguably important in any system of ITE and provide an essential basis in terms of approaches and procedures and theoretical knowledge, for those who work with student teachers. Like all fields of study it is evolving, but its central thrust, as expressed for example by Reid in 1979, is still clear. Its focus is on practical problems and its processes are founded on practical reasoning (see Reid 1979, especially Chapters 3 and 4).

This commitment of Curriculum Studies − which has been developing since the mid-1970s − makes it all the more ironic that tutors' knowledge has been presented as if it is still uninterested in and unhelpful to the refinement of practice.

Tutors' knowledge successfully challenged

Amongst others then a considerable list of reasons might be advanced for the demise of the tutor. They all in a sense show how the tutor's knowledge has been successfully challenged by government for its own ideological ends. They include the following:

- the changes in Education Studies and the admission that earlier approaches were inadequate (though this is no different from all developments and changes that have happened in education in the last twenty years)

- the strong memory in school colleagues of the inadequacy of the theoretical parts of their course and the failure to show that changes had been made to this

- the too submissive response by education departments to government calls for simpler skills-based approaches (which raises again issues about academic freedom and autonomy)

- the acceptance of demands by government for tutors to gain recent and relevant experience of schools, thereby accepting governmental definitions of the role of the tutor instead of being able to demonstrate the importance of a different role

- the parallel appointment of young staff with recent and relevant *school* experience but little experience of the traditions of scholarship in HE (and the failure to offer them appropriate staff development in this area)

- the apparent inability of or lack of priority for tutors to articulate their tacit knowledge and to explain to the profession and the partners their expertise and roles

- the (proper) concern of tutors with uncertain and contestable questions rather than simple training instructions has, in an age which looks for certainty, made it seem that they offer little that is practical.

In the face of all of this (some of it arguably deliberate manipulation of public understanding; some of it plain failure by HE to convey the character of current university courses), it is hardly surprising that there is so much ignorance or misconception about the tutor's current contribution to the preparation of future members

24

of the teaching profession. And as a result of this, tutors have gradually found the conditions in which they work alien to the development and refinement of it. Yet, equally, it is this very need to challenge, change and develop educational understanding that confirms the place of the study of education in the democratic university setting.

Some questions for the partners

Before turning to the details of the examples of tutors' work readers may wish to ponder the following questions, many of which they may wish to take with them into the next sections of the book.

1. What are my own personal experiences of Education Studies in my initial training and do I assume that it is still being offered in colleges?

2. Can I see where they fit in the history offered above?

3. What assumptions do I make about the HE tutor and his/her role?

4. What do I actually know about what happens in college in the ITE course today?

5. What kinds of things do I want to find out about the tutor and the HE dimension?

References

Barrett, E., (1992) *Initial teacher education in England and Wales: a topography (The Modes of Teacher Education Survey)*. London: Goldsmiths College.
Bekhradnia, B. (1994) 'Buffer body with good track record', *Times Higher Educational Supplement* (27.5.94), p.13.
Bullough, R. and Gitlin, A. (1994) 'Challenging teacher education as training: four propositions', *Journal of Education for Teaching,* **20** (1), pp.67 – 81.
CATE (1986) *Catenote 4*. London: CATE.
DES (1983a) *Teaching in schools: the content of initial training*. London: DES.
DES (1983b) *Teaching quality (White Paper)*. London: HMSO.
DES (1984) *Initial teacher training: approval of courses (Circular 3/84)*. London: DES.
DES (1988) *Qualified teacher status: a consultation document*. London: DES.

25

DES (1989) *Initial teacher training: approval of courses (Circular 24/89)*. London: DES.
DFE (1992) *Initial teacher training (secondary phase) (Circular 9/92)*. London: DFE.
DFE (1993) *The initial training of primary school teachers: new criteria for courses (Circular 14/93)*. London: DFE.
Eraut, M. (1989) 'Initial teacher training and the National Vocational Qualifications model' in Burke, J. (Ed.) (1989) *Competency-based education and training*. London: Falmer, pp.171–85.
Fish, D. (1989) *Learning through practice in initial teacher training*. London: Kogan Page.
Fish, D. (1995) *Quality mentoring for student teachers: a principled approach to practice*. London: David Fulton.
Frayling, C. (1994) 'Artefacts rather than facts' *Times Higher Education Supplement* (20.5.94), p.9.
Gardner, P. (1993) 'The early history of school-based teacher training', in McIntrye, D., Haggar, H. and Wilkin, M. (1993) *Mentoring: perspectives on school-based teacher education*. London: Kogan Page, pp.21–36.
Gilroy, P. (1993) 'Reflections on Schön: an epistemological critique and a practical alternative', in Gilroy, P. and Smith, M. (Eds) (1993) *International Analysis of Teacher Education: Journal of Education for Teaching*, **19** (4/5), pp.83–9.
Griffiths, M. and Tann, S. (1992) 'Using reflective practice to link personal and public theories', *Journal of Education for Teaching*, **18** (1) pp.69–84.
Kelly, A.V. (1993) 'Education as a field of study in a university: challenge, critique, dialogue, debate', *Journal of Education for Teaching*, **19** (2), pp.125–39.
Kydd, L. and Weir, D. (1993) 'Initial teacher training: the professional route to technician status', *British Journal of Educational Studies*, **41** (3), pp.400–11.
Loder, C. (1990) 'The introduction of staff appraisal in universities as a method of quality assurance', in Loder, C. (Ed.) (1990) *Quality assurance and accountability in higher education* (The Bedford Way Series). London: Kogan Page, pp.42–54.
Moses, I. (1989) 'Role and problems of heads of departments in performance appraisal', *Assessment and Evaluation in Higher Education*, **14** (2) pp.95–105.
Nance, D. and Fawns, R. (1993) 'Teachers' working knowledge and training: the Australian agenda for the reform of teacher education', *Journal of Education for Teaching*, **19** (2) pp.159–74.
Oakeshott, M. (1972) 'Education: the engagement and its frustration', in Dearden, R.F., Hirst, P.H. and Peters, R.S. (Eds) (1972) *Education and the development of reason*. London: Routledge and Kegan Paul, pp.19–49.
Reid, W. (1979) *Thinking about the curriculum: the nature and treatment of curriculum problems*. London: Routledge and Kegan Paul.
Schnur, J. and Golby, M. (1995, in press) 'Teacher education: a university mission?', *Journal of Teacher Education*, **46** (1).
Stones, E. (1992) *Quality teaching: a sample of cases*. London: Routledge.

Taylor, W. (1994) 'Quality assurance', in Wilkin, M. and Sankey, D. (Eds) (1994) *Collaboration and transition in initial teacher training.* London: Kogan Page, pp.161–73.

Wilkin, M. (1990) 'The development of partnership in the United Kingdom', in Booth, M., Furlong, J. and Wilkin, M. (Eds) (1990) *Partnership in initial teacher training.* London: Cassell, pp.3–23.

Williams, G. (1990) 'Quality and resource allocation', in Loder, C. (Ed.) (1990) *Quality assurance and accountability in higher education* (The Bedford Way Series). London: Kogan Page, pp.72–82.

CHAPTER 2

Enquiring into the Tutor's Role: Present Practice and Future Potential

Introduction

The following studies show tutors at work within both undergraduate and postgraduate ITE courses at what was called West London Institute, and which has since become part of Brunel University. These particular courses were, at the time being portrayed, all traditionally designed, in the sense that they were not yet required to be 'reformed' under *Circulars 9/92* or *14/93*, and thus still retained a *balanced* partnership between tutors and teachers over matters including teaching practice.

The focus of these studies is the work of the tutor. Elsewhere in all the ITE offered by the Institute there were parts of courses where teachers and tutors worked very closely together, but that closeness renders the evidence we wish to focus on more complex, and the tutor's role less visible, and so tutors were asked to share with the reader studies of themselves working in a central role with students.

All the courses represented here were based on a reflective practice philosophy. (See Chapter 1 and also Fish (1995) for more detail on the thinking behind this approach.) The implications of this philosophy are that teachers (and this includes tutors) should investigate and reflect upon the evidence of their practices with a view to refining, developing or changing them in the light of their enquiries, reading, writing, collegiate deliberations and further thought. The time and resources for writing these studies were provided by research monies won for the Institute as a result of the publication of earlier research which was itself conducted entirely in addition to full working timetables, (for example, Catt and Sweeney 1992; Fish 1989; Fish *et al.* 1990 and 1991; and Sweeney and Catt 1993).

Enquiring into present practice

Investigations or, more grandly, research activities, which seek to provide the base for reflective practice and which therefore involve small-scale enquiry by the professional into his/her own practice, are inevitably conducted from within what is known as the humanistic, interpretative paradigm. In this, the approach is case study and the tools are drawn mainly from the arts and sociology, but it is an open question what methods should be used in any given study. Indeed, Golby argues that 'case study, properly conceived, is uniquely appropriate as a form of educational research for practitioners to conduct' (Golby 1993, p.3) and is 'synonymous with professional activity; it is what professionals do day by day' (Golby 1993, p.11). The hallmark of case study is not having a body of knowledge about practice but knowing how to access the knowledge necessary to enlighten particular cases.

Case studies are 'strong in reality'; they are complex, messy, at times contradictory, yet these accounts can make telling connections within practitioners' experiences. A case study is an empirical enquiry which investigates contemporary real life events using multiple sources of evidence. It is, Golby argues, 'appropriate where it is not yet clear what are the right questions to ask', but where there is 'a sense of perplexity, problems to be addressed, and a sense of the researcher's interest in those problems'. A case, he suggests, 'must always be a case, or example, of something' seen in relation to a wider set of ideas. It starts from a provisional understanding and investigates it further (see Golby 1993, pp.5–6). It is not a study of uniqueness but of particularity. The *unique* event, as Elton says, is 'a freak and a frustration ... it lacks every measurable dimension and cannot be assessed' (quoted in Golby 1993, p.8), whereas an event that is *particular* is like other events of similar kind but is not identical to them. Generalisation is achieved through a sense of the representativeness or typicality of the case.

The language of case studies avoids the specialised terminology and assumptions of other research methods, enabling readers to judge the implications for themselves. And studies are presented so that readers are in a position to consider alternative interpretations whilst receiving a particular view. Case study data is difficult to organise, but such studies offer the opportunity to look in detail at practice and consider it closely. Case studies are embedded in action and contribute to further action in terms of professional development. Presented in Section 2 below, then, are small-scale case studies of HE tutors at work with students in a range of contexts, written by those who have investigated their own practice. They thus represent aspects of HE tutors' practice. The tools they have chosen suit both the nature of the investigation and the pragmatic possibilities of the practice being studied. In particular they were: situation analysis; video and tape recordings and transcripts; semi-structured interviews; and documentary evidence (from tutors' own paperwork and often also from students' writings on teaching practice or in course assignments or student evaluations of the unit of work). Drawing upon these, they offer vignettes, stories, film-shots – even the dramas – of their practice. By these means they seek to capture and present the rich texture of their work with students in order to gain insight into the processes of their own and students' professional development. They offer details (inevitably subjectively selected) of actions, feelings, motives, conversations, whilst properly maintaining confidentiality.

Yet the data they have gathered does not over-dominate their thinking. Essentially they are concerned to stand back from it and to understand, to think, to clarify. Their approach is tentative. They seek to explore, and learn, rather than to prove or disprove. They attempt to 'get inside a piece of teaching to shed light on the process' (see below, p. 115). They are prepared to share their uncertainties in order to extend their own learning. Following Schön (1987), they offer the flavour of reflection-in-action (the thoughts of tutor or student as they think on their feet during action) and reflection-on-action (the considerations and speculations that result from looking back over practice in a systematic way). They are sharply conscious of their own techniques in both the teaching and the investigations of it, and they are not afraid to reveal them.

Clearly, therefore, they are not seeking to hold up their studies as examples of good practice, but as ways of learning about practice. Nor are their studies here presented in order to establish some overall universal statements about good practice for the tutor. Indeed, we believe with Alexander that 'good practice is identified and achieved dialectically and empirically, not by decree' (Alexander 1990, p.72), and that it is context specific. Their aspirations are therefore at once both humble and yet significant, their intentions simple and yet complex. As a result they highlight and report details which might easily be seen by others as essentially trivial and insignificant, and they demonstrate how by attending to these they develop their own and students' ideas and practices. In short, they help us to see students' learning and tutors' teaching anew. And in that way, as we shall see, they are working towards the same goals that shape their work with students. By offering us rich descriptions 'aimed at capturing and disclosing the culturally embedded meanings of [their own] classroom events' (Reid 1979, p.34), they parallel what they seek from students − and work to the same end.

The studies

All the following studies show tutors at work with student teachers. The range of courses and the range of a tutor's involvement in initial teacher education is demonstrated by the set of studies as a whole, since each study focusses on a different part of a tutor's role. Thus, we follow one who supervises a student on teaching practice, we hear of work with students in schools on day visits, and we see a range of different work in the college setting in different subject areas, and age-range specialisms. It should also be noted that tutors often work across several ITE courses and at the same time carry out other duties in respect of in-service work, research and (though not a focus of this book) administration. Some have come from advisory work in local education authorities (LEAs); some have held senior posts in schools. Their own autobiographical details are provided in the Notes on Contributors at the front of the book (page vii above). The brief they were given was to share a piece of their practice in ITE which illuminated an aspect of their role as an education tutor. No further limitations were placed upon the work. The following provides a brief summary of the studies.

In Chapter 3, 'Just a Nod and a Wink: Collaborative Skills Developed in Collaborative Ways with Early Years Student Teachers', Hilma Rask focusses on ways in which undergraduate and graduate primary student teachers can be enabled to develop collaborative skills which can support effective teamwork in the classroom. She investigates three perspectives: those of the successful and experienced class teacher, of the student, and of her own view as the HE tutor. The college course and the school classroom are both shown to play a vital role, and the tutor's chance to investigate across them is shown to enrich them both.

In Chapter 4, 'Student Voices: "A Lot of Theory Jammed into their Brain"?', Robert Catt and Tom Sweeney present a detailed examination of a single aspect of an undergraduate secondary Educational Studies programme and provide an incidental view of the collaborative practice of two college lecturers involved in planning and teaching the programme. Following a contextual outline they draw data from a unit of work on 'classroom management', with some additional reference to a complementary unit, 'communicating in the classroom'. They offer some detailed commentary upon transcribed extracts from a seminar and attempt to provide an illuminative evaluation of critical features of their essentially reflective practice in ITE. While their work combines the perspectives of college tutors, school teachers and students, it demonstrates some specialist teaching strategies which give students in HE opportunities and time to find a voice and develop their own theories as teachers in the making.

Christine Edwards illustrates practice with primary graduate and undergraduate student teachers who are non-specialists in music, in Chapter 5: **'Music Today – and Tomorrow?'** She conveys the flavour of arts work in HE's teacher preparation courses. She shows an attempt to maintain a balance between offering students tried-and-tested curriculum ideas for use in the classroom, and providing them with creative work at their own level which allows for a great variety of competence, and develops their confidence and skills. This chapter demonstrates the importance of providing opportunities for reflection and analysis, and concludes by asking whether the resources and opportunities she describes will still be available under school-centred ITT.

In contrast to this, in Chapter 6: **'"Pin your Thoughts on the Wall": The Role of Display in the Classroom'**, Lynne Thorogood draws upon a study of a postgraduate primary student teacher and a tutor discovering the power of display to motivate difficult pupils in a Key Stage 2 classroom. She shows how subsequent investigations in a secondary school with a practising teacher draw attention to the power of the signs embedded in classroom display. She draws conclusions about the particular and the generalisable in ITE, and the essentially seamless nature of teacher education as opposed to the traditional divisions between ITE and in-service work.

Finally, in Chapter 7: **'Enquiring into the Arts: Teaching Drama to Students and to Pupils'**, Tom Sweeney and Robert Catt focus upon the Creative Arts and offer a rich case study of a drama project in which two tutors work with a class of Year 6 pupils and a class of PGCE primary students. They show how, subsequently, their work provided a basis for a topic for a student on teaching practice. The tutors involved critically evaluate the entire unit of their work in relation to the development of understanding and of enquiry skills amongst the students. They also comment on the

32

value of collaborative inquiry as part of the teaching and learning process and on arts and their role in the curriculum.

In all cases the studies speak clearly for themselves, and need no editorial comments and no additional notes. However, in order to ensure that the reader who does not work in an HE setting has access to the overall context of the studies, the following section offers some brief details about the courses, their ethos and their operation. But it should be noted that most of the issues presented in the studies below are generic issues and require no detailed knowledge or understanding of these courses beyond what the authors themselves offer.

Some background details

Our particular education department, like many in the country, offers primary and secondary ITE courses and offers them both as undergraduate and graduate routes.

Thus, when these studies were written, the Institute (now part of Brunel University) offered at secondary level, for those wishing to teach the eleven to eighteen age range, a one-year full-time graduate (PGCE) secondary course (already under *Circular 9/92* regulations), and available in geography, physical education, religious education, English and modern foreign languages, with supportive education as a subsidiary subject. It also offered a four-year undergraduate Bachelor of Arts or of Science Honours degree with Qualified Teacher Status (BA/BSc/QTS) in physical education or geography and environmental issues, with English, religious studies or information technology as subsidiary subjects. This used to be called a Bachelor of Education (BEd). In this degree course the final two years focussed essentially on education but the first two years were mainly subject study. (This is referred to as a '2+2' course.) For their subject study, students took units of an Integrated Degree Scheme including a wide range of BA and BSc subjects. They studied their subjects in class with those taking pure degrees in those subjects. This scheme worked on a semester base with two semesters per year (September to February and February to June) with fifteen weeks per semester. In each week students were taught across three modules for the equivalent of a day per module. The rest of their time was spent reading, writing and preparing for, or operating in, the school classroom. Some modules were education-focussed in the first two years, but most of the school-based and school-focussed modules were offered in the third and fourth years.

The primary education pattern was very similar. There was a primary PGCE with age range specialisms in the five to nine, or the seven to eleven age ranges. This prepared students to teach the National Curriculum in primary schools and to take a professional studies project in a specialism drawn from the core or foundation subjects of the National Curriculum. The BA/QTS four-year undergraduate primary course offered specialisms in the three to seven, five to eight, or seven to eleven age ranges, but this specialist age-range focus operated only in the third and fourth years of the course. All work in school in the first two years of the course provided experience of all age ranges. This course was, like the four-year secondary course, part of the Integrated Degree Scheme, and students could follow degree subjects in either a Creative Arts or an Environmental Studies cluster of subjects. These students were prepared to teach every subject of the National Curriculum, but they specialised slightly more in the teaching of the subject areas in which they also took their degree modules, and rather less in the subjects from the other cluster. Hence, Christine Edwards' chapter is about working on music in the classroom with students who specialised in environmental studies subjects like history, geography or religious studies.

All four courses had practical work in school at the centre of all their education work. Thus all work in college either looked towards work about to happen in school or looked back on work completed. The college-based modules or parts of modules focussed on three aspects: the teaching of particular ages ('age-range work'); the teaching of National Curriculum subjects (curriculum work); and the study of education (Education Studies/Professional Studies/Theory and Practice modules). It is perhaps significant in the light of the comments made about Education Studies in Chapter 1 above, that it was this aspect of courses which is referred to in the most disparate terms across courses.

Work in school was both in teaching practice (TP) blocks (also called sustained school experience) and regular day visits to non-TP schools, referred to as 'serial experience' by the secondary teams and as 'intermittent school experience' amongst primary courses. All teaching practices were preceded by a series of day visits to the TP school. TPs were all assessed. Preparation for work in school was extensive and careful. The TP file was seen as central to students' learning through practice, and diaries of practical work were also used to help students reflect. Indeed, the roles of both writing and talking in students' learning was given careful attention. For this reason, most of the students' written assignments in education work were centred on understanding practice and practical problems. All students wrote an extended study based on work in school. The undergraduates' version of this was called a 'special exercise'. It was the final piece of work on the course, synthesised their understanding of relationships between theory and practice and counted for twice as many marks as each of their other essays. In all but the secondary PGCE, tutors were still working with teachers on TP supervision when these studies were written because the other three courses were not yet under the new regulations. In this role, tutors were often consulted by both students and teachers – sometimes together, sometimes independently – about matters both professional and personal.

With these details in mind then, and with the questions below as a focus, it is time to turn to the studies themselves.

Future potential

These studies offer particular cases of the HE tutor at work. But their ultimate significance lies in their representative typicality. Since the work of HE tutors in Education has not been well documented, these studies provide an important opportunity to *begin* to understand aspects of such work better. In order, therefore, better to consider the emerging issues about the role and practices of education tutors in these cases and their informing theoretical perspectives, I both considered the case studies in detail and also discussed them at length in a workshop with all the writers, where I invited them to consider their personal theories (the theories-in-use) and to compare them with those theories they claim influenced their work (their espoused theories). I also considered other formal theoretical perspectives on practice drawn from a range of sources. From that work I have sought to consider some common themes across the studies, highlight some broad aspects of HE tutors' educational practices and, as a result, to indicate issues for further investigation. There is no attempt here to offer arbitrary generalisations from what have always been considered as specific cases. The aim, rather, is to make a small contribution to a debate which must draw upon wider examples, and which the current climate makes crucial to the survival of an HE dimension in ITE.

Some questions to ask as you read

The following questions might be asked of each study as you read. They are also worth asking across studies. Since many of these important issues about these tutors' work are generic and not age-range or subject specific, readers are recommended to read all the studies and not just those relating to their own specialist interests.

1. How do tutors see their contribution to the education of student teachers?

2. What, exactly (or as exactly as possible), are their intentions for their work with students and in their presentation of it here?

3. What do the studies show about tutors' skills and strategies?

4. What constitutes their knowledge-base?

5. What assumptions, beliefs, values and theories underlie their practices?

6. What are their views about *what* students should learn?

7. What are their views of *how* students actually learn?

8. What patterns recur across the studies, and what might be their significance?

References

Alexander, R. (1990) 'Partnership in initial teacher education: confronting the issues', in Booth, M. *et al*. (Eds) (1990) *Partnership in initial teacher training*. London: Cassell, pp.59–73.

Catt, R. and Sweeney, T. (1992) 'Mythical theory', *Education* (7.2.92), p.110.

DFE (1992) *Initial teacher training (secondary phase) (Circular 9/92)*. London: DFE.

DFE (1993) *The initial training of primary school teachers: new criteria for courses (Circular 14/93)*. London: DFE.

Fish, D. (1989) *Learning through practice in initial teacher training*. London: Kogan Page.

Fish, D. (1995) *Quality mentoring for student teachers: a principled approach to practice*. London: David Fulton.

Fish, D., Twinn, S. and Purr, B. (1990) *How to enable learning through professional practice*. London: West London Press.

Fish, D., Twinn, S. and Purr, B. (1991) *Promoting reflection: improving the supervision of practice in health visiting and initial teacher training*. London: West London Institute.

Golby, M. (1993) *Case study as educational research*. Tiverton: Fair Way Publications.

Reid, W. (1979) *Thinking about the curriculum: the nature and treatment of curriculum problems*. London: Routledge and Kegan Paul.

Schön, D. (1987) *Educating the reflective practitioner*. London: Jossey Bass.

Sweeney, T. and Catt, R. (1993) 'Is there any point?' *Education* (19.3.93), pp.210–11.

Part 2

Educating Student Teachers: Illuminating Tutors' Practices

CHAPTER 3

Just a Nod and a Wink: Collaborative Skills Developed in Collaborative Ways with Early Years Student Teachers

Hilma Rask

Introduction

This chapter presents two complementary case studies which chart some of the processes of professional growth which took place for two student teachers in the area of collaborative teamwork within nursery settings. The taught course and the period of sustained school experience are both shown to play a vital role, and the tutor's chance to investigate across them is seen to be professionally enriching. Both students were undertaking a full-time four-year BA/QTS course. They were on the primary teaching course and had elected to work with the three to seven age range as their specialism during the final two years of the course. This necessitated a five-week period of sustained school experience in a nursery class during their third year. My work as an early years tutor on the course involved a twelve-week preparatory teaching module of three hours each week with students who were to undertake nursery placements. In addition to this programme, the students were involved in other taught sessions in either Creative Arts or Environmental Studies, according to their own areas of selected specialist studies within the

BA/QTS route. I also acted as the college supervisor during the sustained school experience which is presented in the case studies.

Recent literature has highlighted the need for ITE courses to equip early years students with a range of effective management and interpersonal skills for working with adults (Curtis and Hevey 1992; David 1990; Dowling 1992; Hurst 1991; Lally 1991). David (1993) suggests that little attention appears to have been given to preparing student teachers for working with adults at ITE level generally within the United Kingdom. She highlights the fact that the nursery teacher is simultaneously required to be involved in team management within her own particular workplace and to contribute as a member of a team within other multi-professional contexts. It is clearly important to recognise the increasingly multi-professional nature of the framework of provision for young children and the need for ever closer liaison between the many agencies involved in both care and education (Rumbold Report 1990). Such scenarios require considerable interpersonal and managerial skills on the part of the nursery teacher in particular. Yeomans offers a sharp reminder that:

> developing the skills of working with adults is as important a part of the preparation of early years teachers as is concern with working with children, since the two are inextricably linked.
> (Yeomans 1989, p.26)

Research undertaken in a range of nursery settings in Salford (Burgess *et al.* 1989) highlights the stressful role conflicts experienced by both nursery teachers and headteachers as they struggle to balance their dual roles of teachers and managers. The policy implications of this research are far-reaching. A further indication is that a range of managerial skills are required by nursery teachers from a very early stage in their careers (Moxon *et al.* 1991). To neglect this area in ITE courses could add to role conflict and accompanying stress.

Ways have been sought to place awareness of the complexities involved in working in collaboration with other adults in the classroom firmly on the agenda as a part of our taught early years course. However, there are considerable constraints upon the time which can be given over to this due to the tensions of hourage requirements for the various curriculum areas which exist on primary teacher education courses. One of the teaching sessions which sets out to explore issues surrounding working with adults involves small group discussions and role-play exercises. These exercises outline possible scenarios in early years classroom contexts and invite group and individual explorations of possible actions and consequences of such actions. Sessions such as this aim to provide a safe place in which to take risks and to explore, in a more considered way, approaches to dealing with adults in a team setting. Contexts described may include dealing with adult confrontation, negotiating change, managing a difficult or distressed parent or working with an entrenched colleague. Hall and Hall propose that such experiential exercises aim 'to facilitate changes in awareness and to practise new ways of responding to situations' (see Hall and Hall 1988, p.77).

Yeomans (1989) argues that the nature of the partnership between teachers and nursery nurses might best be described as 'a partnership of unequals' in early years classrooms and urges teacher educators to prepare student teachers more fully for this important relationship. David (1990) also highlights the complexities inherent in working relationships between teachers and nursery nurses. Certainly issues of status, pay, responsibilities and power relationships continue to merit a closer investigation within nursery settings for researchers. It is interesting to reflect on the fact that, during sustained school experience in the nursery, the student will be taking many cues from her more experienced nursery nurse colleagues. It can be a daunting prospect for a student teacher to develop a leadership role within such a context. It is, however, clearly crucial that school experience placements should offer student teachers opportunities to begin to grapple with managerial responsibilities, if they are to understand fully their professional roles.

The network of effective partnerships which build up between schools, students and HEIs are all vital contributory factors in facilitating professional growth for the students during sustained school experience. Hodgkinson (1993) offers an interesting analysis of the complexities involved in such diverse partnership arrangements and pinpoints different ways in which individual students may experience and interpret the personal relationships which are involved between the different parties.

The notion of reflection being in a sense an 'ongoing conversation' (Adler, 1991) fits well with the voices which emerge from the case studies presented. Written evaluations of daily practice, which the students maintained in their files, provide a rich resource and offer powerful first-hand illustrations of their experience of collaborative teamwork. Incidents emerging may appear at first glance to be insignificant and responses to be cautiously explored at times. However, I hope to illustrate that, when fully attended to, it is these small events which provide deep and lasting consequences for future practice. I was fortunate to have the opportunity to conduct semi-structured interviews with the two student teachers nine months after the nursery school experience had taken place. This gave me the chance to follow up and explore their longer-term reflections on the teamwork experience. By this time both students had successfully completed their final period of sustained school experience in infant classrooms. Transcripts of the taped interviews which took place have been utilised in order that the voices of the students can continue to emerge, offering honest and engaging debate on the issues surrounding collaborative teamwork and their own leadership roles.

When describing the development of a particularly dynamic and committed team of co-workers in an under-fives centre, Whalley (1992) points out that 'working as a team is a process not a technique'. It is to the exploration of that process which the focus of this chapter will now turn.

Student voices from the nursery: two case studies

Introductory biographies of the students

Both Jenny and Elizabeth were mature students and parents themselves. They were both juggling with the complex demands of full-time study and busy family lives. Jenny had previously trained as a nursery nurse. Both students came to the school placement with successful previous experience in schools. They had shown real enthusiasm for the age-range component of the taught course and asked questions about their own practice with children. They had both displayed good collaborative skills in group tasks and presentations during the taught course, which had prepared them for the nursery placement.

The school settings

Both placements were in nursery classes attached to infant schools in the same borough and both nurseries reflected elements of the High Scope approach as their underpinning philosophy for working with young children (Hohmann, Banet and Weikart 1979). This involved a routine of 'plan, do and review' during the session. The model included the use of small-group time and circle times, when teachers and children sat together to plan and, later, review activities undertaken.

Nursery A consisted of excellent purpose-built accommodation which was well designed and well resourced. It was housed in a separate building to the main school and had a pleasant outdoor play area. It was inviting, attractive and welcoming. This nursery catered for two groups of children in both morning and afternoon sessions and was composed of a team of two full-time nursery teachers and two full-time nursery nurses. Jenny's teacher was the teacher in charge of the nursery. This was a team which worked very much in unison, as each member of staff had responsibility for a 'home group' at certain points in the day, and planned activities were available for all the children.

Nursery B was housed in accommodation adapted from the original infant classrooms and playground. This being so, although it was spacious, friendly and welcoming, it was not as well designed nor as well resourced as nursery A. This nursery catered for both a morning and an afternoon session although there were more children in the morning session than in the afternoon one. It was staffed by a nursery teacher and two nursery nurses, one of whom worked only in the mornings. Members of staff worked closely together, but here the teacher and nursery nurses joined together for circle times, and each member of staff took on responsibilities for a different indoor or outdoor area on a rotational basis.

Both nursery classes were run by excellent and committed practitioners with much experience of working with very young children and with leading a team of adults. Parent helpers were much in evidence in both classes in addition to visiting specialist support teachers.

Case Study 1: Jenny's story

This section presents some of the events which took place during the period of the sustained school experience which Jenny undertook in nursery A. It is illustrated with examples drawn from Jenny's file, in which she evaluated her own progress and reflected on her experiences of teamwork and the leadership role.

Before starting the school experience placement all students had made a series of visits to the nursery. They were required to attend at least one team planning meeting before the start of their placement in order to observe the ways in which the teacher and nursery nurse discussed their plans together. Jenny had duly attended preliminary team meetings and had gained a clear understanding of the High

Scope model which shaped the structure of the curriculum in this nursery. She also knew that she would be setting up a learning environment which would be shared by the other groups of children during the 'plan, do and review' cycle. Jenny knew that she was expected to take an active role in the team meetings and had conscientiously formulated her plans for the period of the school experience.

The first team meeting during the placement arrived, and Jenny was given the opportunity to present her plans to the team. Unfortunately, due to a genuine misunderstanding, both parties had imagined that the other would set the agenda for presenting the plans. The class teacher stepped back from her role as team leader, and Jenny floundered as best she could. She was glad when the meeting ended. Her confidence was considerably shaken, but she was aware that something valuable had been learned. She vowed that she would always be prepared for team meetings, with a clear agenda to hand. Jenny's teacher was equally distressed, since she had intended to be supportive by giving an opportunity for the plans to be presented. Her apologies were profuse as soon as she realised that there had been a misunderstanding. As the supervisor for the placement, I was given accounts of what had taken place, and we were able to discuss future arrangements. Jenny's teacher shared with both Jenny and myself that something valuable had come out of this unfortunate incident for her as well. In future she intended to ensure that the chairing of team meetings would be rotated from time to time to give experience to all members of the team. She had been made aware of the professional value of this for everyone.

During the following week, agenda firmly by her side, Jenny contributed towards a very successful meeting to present and discuss her plans with the rest of the team. She gained a great deal of confidence as a result, and her class teacher was full of encouragement and support.

However, Jenny was soon to be confronted with a serious family problem and arrived one morning feeling very anxious and stressed. It was commendable that she was actually there at all. She commented in her file:

> Hadn't been able to share it with the team. There's no time for chit-chat, just a short good morning and we're busy preparing for the day.

Jenny had intended to plan out particular management strategies for dealing with disruptive behaviour in one area of the nursery but had not been able to do so, due to her personal circumstances. She ended up by 'getting cross' with the children which was inappropriate and left her feeling unhappy and disappointed. She was aware that her new colleagues were also disappointed. It was not until the end of the day that Jenny was able to share her feelings of stress and anxiety with the team. Their support was immediate. They explained that trusting and supporting each other was an integral part of the team spirit in this workplace. In other words, they told Jenny that she was of consequence, that they cared and that caring human relationships were at the heart of their professional practice. Jenny wrote:

> On reflection I should have let the team know my feelings because after discussing it later I felt much better in myself.

It was a mark of her professionalism that Jenny continued to give the school experience her full attention despite a continuing time of personal anxiety. As her confidence grew she was to write:

> I feel much happier with my role within the team. I am feeling more confident in the team planning meetings, although there are still areas I need to reflect on further.

Increasingly her comments and daily evaluations, I noticed, included the term 'we' rather than 'I', which speaks powerfully of a growing awareness of the nature of collaborative teamwork and the need to involve and listen to others.

> I planned it so that there should be interaction and *we've* decided that, as it is a short week next week, *we* will leave it, but gradually incorporate other objects [my italics].

After a planning meeting about midway through the school experience, Jenny was able to write that she felt more confident in her own role and clearer on the roles of the rest of the team. She felt more confident in chairing a meeting and was less afraid of 'treading on people's toes'. It was clear during my visits that Jenny had become a part of the team and was valued for her contributions to the nursery. She looked increasingly critically at her own attitudes as a team member. She had identified a tendency to keep problems to herself to solve but found that these could be aired,

46

debated and worked out through discussion within the team. She noted in her file that this was both constructive and valid.

Jenny realised that her opinion was being valued within the team and noticed that colleagues were not afraid to offer her constructive criticism.

> I've been approached with queries, as well as criticisms over activities, but positively. 'It hasn't worked like this, how about that way?', for example.

Some particularly imaginative activities were planned by Jenny which fully exploited the use of the outdoor area. This aroused enthusiasm from the team and her position was very much strengthened as a result. Jenny made a note towards the end of the placement that:

> The planning meeting went without any hitches and they started discussing and asking me about the following week and I had to remind them that this was my last week coming up.

In the final week of the placement a half-termly evaluation meeting took place, chaired by the teacher, and in a rare moment of self-congratulation Jenny wrote:

> I felt very encouraged after the planning and evaluation meeting. I know I have learned a lot, especially about team work and leadership, but it was nice to hear that I wasn't too hard to work with and that the ideas I had brought in were different and refreshing and had given them ideas for extension activities. I feel after this practice I can be more assertive, yet not feel that I'm being very bossy or pushy.

Jenny had clearly begun to find her voice. She had begun to grapple with the complex nature of collaborative teamwork which involves listening, sharing, supporting each other's contributions and negotiating ways forward as a team. She now appeared to have a growing assurance in her ability to take on an effective managerial role in such a setting.

Case Study 2: Elizabeth's story

This section offers a second case study which complements the first. It is also concerned with the development of a student teacher's understanding of the nature of collaborative teamwork in the nursery. What is unique about this case is the way in which, through reflection on time management, the student starts to question principles underlying her practice and to explore ways of negotiating change. As in the first case study, illustrations are drawn from the student's file.

Within the first week of the placement Elizabeth had pinpointed one of the organisational difficulties which the design of the accommodation brought about. She had to designate staff responsibilities for different areas of the nursery to both the nursery nurses. In addition to this, two trainee nursery nurses were making weekly visits into the nursery. These students were working under the direction of the class teacher but, inevitably, became involved in the curriculum planned by Elizabeth. Careful planning and co-ordination was of the essence in such a setting.

At an early stage in the placement, Elizabeth identified that the management and use of time was of crucial importance. She found that her own timing was running persistently late, and she took herself to task on this issue.

> On reflection I see the vital importance of time keeping especially when working in a team. The needs of other team members must be considered. Bad timing disrupts the whole smooth running of the team and might lead to disgruntled staff members.

In this nursery there was no kitchen area and as a consequence staff were released in rotation for a short morning coffee break off site. Elizabeth shared that this was something which she found hard to do.

> For some reason I feel that I have to be there all the time which in fact I don't actually have to do!

We discussed the importance of taking a short break, as Elizabeth acknowledged that whilst working with nursery age children was highly rewarding, it was also physically exhausting.

Elizabeth welcomed her first opportunity to share forward planning with the team. She had plenty of imaginative plans and wanted everyone to become fully involved in these.

> I feel it is vital that we share our ideas. Three heads are better than one. Also each team member knows what they are doing each day.

Elizabeth recognised that the role of the nursery teacher was both more complex and more varied than she had at first realised. She commented on the difficulty which she was experiencing in finding time for individual observations on children:

> because I am usually in the team leader's role and occupied doing something specific.

As the placement developed, Elizabeth saw ways in which communication and collaboration with parents was facilitated. She noted the use of a notice board outside the nursery and began to use this herself to involve parents in the activities which were being provided. Parental interest in her work with the children was evident, and she was able to extend the range of cultural experiences offered to all the children through this. Elizabeth noticed the strong community links which were in place. She commented in her file that such links were clearly vital for quality provision.

During the course of the placement, a student researcher had arranged to visit the nursery. She was looking at issues of time and organisation for young children in different settings. Elizabeth, although somewhat daunted by the prospect, had kindly agreed to the presence of the observer. She was fascinated to discover that the observer was investigating those very same issues of time and organisation which she herself had identified with the team.

> It was interesting that we had already realised and identified the same areas and were grappling with the problems they present.

Elizabeth made careful notes in her file on possible solutions to present to the team following on from her particular concern with the length of time which she was spending with the children in circle time. Planning time was very lengthy since there were so many children in the morning session and individual choices had to be made. We had discussed this, and Elizabeth had been trying to shorten circle time. As she battled towards a solution, Elizabeth was also very much aware of the need to listen to the voices and opinions of the rest of the team.

Another solution might have been to scrap the circle time together and let the children get straight in, but the team seem to feel that it is important to settle the children before the session starts.

Timing and organisation of the day remained a management problem for Elizabeth throughout the placement. She was always ready to blame herself when timing went astray but she did not cease questioning ways in which the situation could be improved. She was aware, however, that changes take time and require considerable negotiation with all parties involved.

> The same old thorny issue of time-keeping and time spent on the mat reared its ugly head again this week. It is obviously an ongoing problem and one which has been discussed many times. As a short time visitor I don't feel able to instigate radical changes. I think the team have already tried a number of approaches.

It was interesting to notice that Elizabeth continued to debate in her own written evaluations advantages and disadvantages of different ways in which the sessions could be organised. She compared this situation with one she had seen during nursery visits on the taught course earlier, which had involved three groups of children working with the teacher and nursery nurses separately during planning time. Elizabeth voiced her dilemma. She wanted to keep to established routines which were consistent with the approach to the curriculum which was being provided, and allowed for the smooth operation of staff coffee breaks. However, she also wanted to allow for the spontaneous moment which she considered to be of vital importance for work with young children.

> I'm making a conscious effort to watch the clock, but it always seems such a shame to stop the children when everyone is happy. I always feel that I have to stick to established routines. It is really in my character to be more spontaneous than to stick to being rigidly organised.

Elizabeth's teacher mentioned to me that her own teacher education course had not addressed management skills for dealing with other adults in the workplace. She considered that this was one of the most important aspects of the nursery teacher's role, and that it was essential for tutors to include it in ITE courses.

At the end of the placement Elizabeth received very positive feedback for the wealth of exciting and innovative activities which she had instigated. All members of the team had appreciated her considerate manner, her warmth and her energy. Elizabeth had experienced at first hand some of the difficulties of negotiating change within a team. She had taken on an admirable role as a leader and had also begun to reflect more deeply on some of her underlying beliefs about ways in which children learn and how a team of adults can best facilitate this. As with my supervision with Jenny, it had been a privilege to witness and contribute to this process of discovery.

Nine months later: continuing stories

Both Jenny and Elizabeth kindly agreed to participate in individual semi-structured interviews about nine months after the completion of their nursery placements. I was interested to explore several areas of continuing interest. First, I wanted to discover more about their longer-term reflections on their experiences of teamwork in the nursery. Second, I wanted to examine any perceived linkages between the taught course and sustained school experience with regard to working in collaboration with others. Finally, I was eager to investigate their current views on the management of a team of adults as they prepared to seek their first appointments in teaching. With their permission the interviews were recorded and subsequently transcribed. By this time I thought that I knew both Jenny and Elizabeth well, and we had a good rapport. The interviews proved to be most enriching for me professionally, since they both demonstrated keen insight into their own personal and professional development. This opened up areas for further reflection on my part, about the nature of ITE and the particular needs of early years student teachers.

Reflections on teamwork

Longer-term reflections on the nursery team experience raised some important aspects on the differences between being an insider and being an outsider. Jenny, when talking about the apparently seamless operation of the team of which she became a part, commented:

> it was all so smooth and you thought, well nothing has been said, so how did you *know* what was happening?

She distinguished between being initially the outsider, and then later the insider, within the team structure. This had necessitated understanding the many non-verbal signals which took place, such as a wave of the hand or facial gestures together with abbreviated comments. It was important to interpret such seemingly small things, for they communicated intentions, actions and decisions amongst members of the team.

Elizabeth mentioned the way in which each member of her team had developed an awareness of just when to intervene in situations between individual children and colleagues. She had found herself learning this too as part of a planned approach to dealing with challenging behaviour from children.

> The thing was never to get upset, never to get uptight. Someone else would take over and it *worked*! Sometimes a child just needed someone else.

Jenny talked with insight on the importance she now placed on sharing problems with colleagues in a team, particularly concerning individual children. She commented on the value of team meetings as a forum for exchanging ideas and observations. She also looked back on the team planning meetings as a most vital learning experience for herself.

> It allowed me the opportunity to take on the role of a team leader and to *have* to think about what the others were going to contribute.

Elizabeth talked at length on how important timing had been during her placement. On reflection, she was aware of just how many constraints had been placed on the team and their daily routines, due to the lack of kitchen facilities and purpose-built accommodation. She mused that the afternoon sessions had been much less fraught.

> We didn't have coffee. There wasn't time. It was all to do with *coffee*!

She was full of praise for her colleague nursery nurses and spoke of their strength and support.

> They looked to me very much for the forward planning and ideas but equally were quite happy to throw in their own ideas and take responsibility.

It was interesting to note that both students spoke in positive ways about the close contacts which they had witnessed between nursery staff and parents. Elizabeth mentioned the fact that her teacher played an important role in the lives of some parents as well as the children. She described her teacher as being like a social worker, community resource and confidante as well as teacher. Jenny remembered back to a moment when a parent had shared something of a confidential nature with her, and she had been entrusted as a professional.

> That really showed me what a powerful relationship teachers and parents can have.

It is to Elizabeth's voice that I will finally turn. She highlights important skills which a student needs to develop in order to work effectively with other adults in a team.

> The experience I had in the third year proved to me that I could work with others and plan for others, and I got to actually thinking about other people doing things at the same time as I was actually doing things.

Linking theory and practice

Several important issues came to the fore during the interviews concerning perceived linkages between theory and practice, school experience and the taught course. It was illuminating to be reminded by both students of the importance of learning through real life experiences. This raised questions on the use of simulation exercises and group tasks during the taught course. To be effective they must be made 'real'. Reality was a word used by both students during interview. Jenny spoke of how her confidence had grown through the school experience:

> because it is a real situation. I think that if it is set up in college, yes, we can work in groups, but it does not somehow have that *reality* about it.

Elizabeth recalled the experience of simulation exercises through outlined scenarios and wryly admitted:

> Yes, all well and good. This is what you *should* do, but when you

are *faced* with a parent! That is another thing altogether. I don't think anything can prepare you for that.

Both students commented positively on the value of group work with fellow students on the taught course. However, there was mention that considerable negotiation skills were required at times, despite this being collaboration between equal partners. Creative Arts productions were considered to have provided valuable team-building experiences. Both the Creative Arts specialist and the non-specialist student had been involved with these during the taught course.

Another outcome of the interviews, was that both students highlighted the importance of developing personal theories throughout the taught course and mentioned how important it was to be aware of underpinning principles of practice. Jenny considered that the taught course offered time to reflect upon and refine developing ideas which arose out of school experience.

You do learn so much being out there, but you need time to come back, to reflect and refine.

Time to reflect on experience gained is something which the taught course aims to offer. Not in an 'ivory tower' sense, but in other ways. A written assignment might be shaped to draw upon issues arising out of practice, or taught sessions built around observations and samples gathered in schools, together with selected personal readings.

Looking to the future

The confident voices of Jenny and Elizabeth during the interviews as they talked about strategies which they would hope to employ as future team leaders, gave powerful testimony to just how far they had individually travelled over the final two years of the course. It was with impressive sensitivity that they both responded when asked about key management strategies which they would adopt if taking up a first appointment in a nursery or reception class.

It would be no good going in and saying, 'Right, we're going to do it this way, because I have learned this at college and this is the way to do it.' You've got to go in and see what is happening, to build on what they are doing that is good practice. Yes, you are going to have your own ideas, but that has got to be negotiated.
First of all you've got to get to know the team. You've got

to sit back and go along with the system to start with and just see where it is, because you can't do a new broom job straight away. I mean, talk to everybody, but if you're the team leader and therefore responsible, if you feel very strongly about something, you've got to find a way of implementing it without ruffling too many feathers. Because that's what you believe in really.

When asked how they might tackle a new colleague who was rather entrenched in attitude, a scenario both students dreaded, responses were carefully considered. Neither student thought that the task would be easy. Diplomacy and tact were viewed as crucial by Elizabeth who was also quick to point out that ultimately a tough line might also be required. She thought that it might be possible to negotiate from the good aspects observed and then find a way forward together. Jenny's words echoed this:

I think that you've got to get alongside them and I think that you've got to value where they are coming from and what good practices they have got. Work on that, work on the positive and the strengths. Then I think there may be a time when you have got to lay it on the line.

I was struck by ways in which these words resonated for me as I reflected on my approach to supervision. These could be the words of a college teaching practice supervisor.

Making connections: issues arising from the case studies

The case studies highlight the value of the written daily evaluations on practice which student teachers are required to maintain during sustained school experience. These serve as an ongoing dialogue about progress over a range of issues to be shared by the student with teachers and supervisors. When evaluations are written with honest critical insight, such records can serve as a source for deeper reflection on their own practice in related contexts by students, teachers and tutors alike.

During the teacher education programme, students currently have opportunities to move between the experience of being in the role of the teacher in the classroom and being a student in

55

a college-based setting. Stepping outside the immediate context of the classroom has an important role. At best in teacher education courses, there exists a constant interplay between the taught course and school experience through which students are encouraged to draw out personal theories from practice. The development of such theoretical underpinnings are crucial for future professional confidence and competence. Indeed, the students in the case studies articulated that this was a fundamental need. David (1990) emphasises the need for nursery teachers to be articulate about the purposes behind their actions if they are to enhance their professional status.

At best the triangular relationship between students, schools and ITE institutions has real strength. The skilled nursery teacher has a wealth of experience of working with adults in her daily work. She and her team, when working in well managed and supportive collaboration, are well placed to contribute to the development of the nursery student teacher. A poorly managed team would not, of course, offer the same support. It is vital, however, that implicit knowledge is made explicit for the student teacher working within a team context. 'A nod and a wink' is clearly far more than it appears in the journey from outsider to insider. It is inevitable that a well established team of co-workers operates a system of abbreviated communications, but it must be remembered that this often serves to shorthand underpinning philosophies about working with young children. Time needs to be made available to explain and share the deeper meanings which lie behind actions and routines during sustained school experience. The tutor has a crucial role here.

A student teacher in the nursery has rapidly to develop a range of effective management strategies for working in collaboration with colleagues in addition to building on existing parent partnerships. Simultaneously the student has to plan appropriate curriculum provision for very young children and create a safe but stimulating learning environment. She has to develop a sufficiently assertive manner to earn the respect and co-operation of her co-workers in order to carry out her plans. Earlier reference was made to the unequal nature of the partnerships which exist between teachers and nursery nurses (Yeomans 1989), but the nursery student teacher is initially the unequal partner during school experience. The nursery nurse has an important role as a collaborating colleague. More account should to be taken of the significance of their valuable support.

There are many tensions surrounding proposed plans for the

emphasis to shift to wholesale school-centred teacher education programmes. Whilst it can be argued that nursery teachers are the very group with considerable experience of managing adults within their role, is it realistic to expect the total responsibility for quality teacher education to fall upon their ever obliging shoulders? Nursery teachers have already been identified as being overstretched. The demands upon their professional time are many and increasingly involve liaison with multi-professional agencies concerned with the education and care of young children. It is vital that school experience placements should provide nursery student teachers with opportunities to extend and develop their range of management skills as a foundation for future professional growth. How can this development best be facilitated?

It is to quality that attention must, in the final analysis, be paid. The HE tutor has an important role within the triangular relationship outlined above. She has the knowledge of the elements contained within the taught course and will, in addition, be likely to have specialist knowledge in specific areas. She is likely to have known the student over a period of time and will have discussed plans with students before placements begin. She can adopt the role of a critical friend as a part of the supervisory role and can liaise with teacher partners to offer reassurance and clarification concerning student progress and placement expectations. Written evaluations on the part of the student are a part of the dialogue which emerges, but above all there must also be critical discussion arising out of practice experience. Such critical talk aims to make explicit connections between theory and practice in action. The HE tutor can facilitate this process in a particularly focussed way.

Nursery education has been painstakingly and collaboratively created over many generations, and it is still in the making. At a time of rapid educational change, it is vital to safeguard underpinning principles which place the child firmly and securely at the centre of his/her curriculum. It has to be remembered, however, that without the continued entry of confident, articulate, innovative and informed teachers who bring with them the beginnings of successful managerial skill and a willingness to collaborate with others, any increased expansion of the nursery sector could be but a hollow victory. It is surely not only a question of 'Starting with Quality' (Rumbold Report 1990), but of ending with quality.

References

Adler, S. (1991) 'The reflective practitioner and the curriculum of teacher education', *Journal of Education for Teaching*, **17** (2), pp.139–50.

Burgess, R.G., Hughes, C. and Moxon, S. (1989) *Educating the under fives in Salford* (Centre for Educational Development, Appraisal and Research Report 1). Coventry: University of Warwick.

Curtis, A. and Hevey, D. (1992) 'Training to work in the early years', in Pugh, G. (Ed.) (1992) *Contemporary issues in the early years: working collaboratively for children*. London: Paul Chapman, in association with the National Children's Bureau, pp.193–210.

David, T. (1990) *Under five – under educated?* Milton Keynes: Open University Press.

David, T. (Ed.) (1993) *Educational provision for our youngest children: European perspectives*. London: Paul Chapman.

DES (1990) *Starting with quality: report of the committee of inquiry into the quality of the educational experiences offered to 3 and 4 year old children (Rumbold Report)*. London: HMSO.

Dowling, M. (1992) *Education 3–5* (2nd edn). London: Paul Chapman.

Hall, E. and Hall, C. (1988) *Human relations in education*. London: Routledge.

High Scope Educational Research Foundation (1986) *Introduction to the High Scope preschool curriculum: a two day workshop*. Ypsilanti, Michigan: High Scope Press.

Hodgkinson, K. (1993) 'Student perceptions of the personal relationships involved in teaching practice in primary schools', *Research in Education* **50** (1), pp.67–82.

Hohmann, M., Banet, B. and Weikart, D. (1979) *Young children in action*. Ypsilanti, Michigan: High Scope Press.

Hurst, V. (1991) *Planning for early learning*. London: Paul Chapman.

Lally, M. (1991) *The nursery teacher in action*. London: Paul Chapman.

Moxon, S., Hughes, C. and Burgess, R.G. (1991) 'It's like a juggler with all the balls in the air . . . : issues of role conflict for headteachers and teachers in nursery schools and centres', *Early Years*, **11** (2), pp.35–7.

Pugh, G. (Ed.) (1992) *Contemporary issues in the early years: working collaboratively for children*. London: Paul Chapman, in association with the National Children's Bureau.

Whalley, M. (1992) 'Working as a team', in Pugh, G. (Ed.) (1992) *Contemporary issues in the early years: working collaboratively for children*. London: Paul Chapman, in association with the National Children's Bureau, pp.157–74.

Yeomans, R. (1989) 'Sustaining a partnership of unequals: colleague relationships in early years contexts', *Early Years*, **10** (1), pp.26–8.

CHAPTER 4

Student Voices: 'A lot of Theory Jammed into their Brain?'

Robert Catt and Tom Sweeney

'I want to see less [sic] teachers coming out of higher education with a lot of theory jammed into their brain.'
John Patten, Secretary of State for Education,
(BBC 1 News, 6/10/93)

Introduction

A considerable gap yawns between, on one side, the popular political rhetoric of the New Right and, on the other, the attempts of those in ITE to work within what is increasingly referred to as a practical curriculum. In this chapter we are aware of the difficulty of finding a middle ground between two manifestly conflicting ideologies. However, we attempt at least to find a tangible footing in a tangled debate through a single case study in ITE which, illustrating the texture of an Educational Studies programme within a four-year undergraduate course for secondary teachers, also gives attention to structural principles and, by the way, provides some view of collaborative practice.

For both of us − writing the chapter and, amongst other time-tabled commitments, teaching an undergraduate Educational Studies programme − the past five years has been a period of disconcerting change in HE. We each entered ITE from a background of considerable experience of teaching in secondary schools − one as a senior teacher, the other as a head of English − and each of us has been struck forcibly and, often, quite personally, by the strident political charge characteristic of the recent period, which denigrates teacher education as 'theoretical' and 'ideological' and in which, increasingly, we have found ourselves caught up. John Patten's Gradgrindian metaphor – more slogan than opinion and employed by us, above, as ironical epigraph rather than solemn epitaph – merely echoes the tiresomely familiar political viewpoint. What we have each found so remarkable is that this apparently popular view of the 'theoretical' way in which teachers are prepared for the profession is so remote from our own practice and that of our colleagues in ITE. Further, and building upon the methodologies we have each found so valuable in school, we find that students, already involved in school-based work, genuinely enjoy our teaching programme and, in their evaluations, comment that it is both stimulating and useful. Although we read about and discuss curriculum and policy, school organisation and classroom teaching, learning and assessment, and we encourage our students, similarly, to read and talk, never have we explicitly regarded our work as mere 'theory'. It is because the seemingly common-sense polemic against the study of Education seems to have such a studied disregard for the working realities of ITE that we have attempted to make sense of events in what, with suitable modesty, we would describe as an enquiry into our own practice. And it is this which we here attempt to share through a series of – borrowing from the terminology of film – 'clips' of our work: beginning with a general structural view or *mise en scène* of the course, cutting to an outline of some selected taught elements before providing a close-up featuring discourse detail from a single lecture session. We shall then conclude the chapter by drawing attention to the principles informing our curriculum design and methodology.

Educational Studies within a four-year course: a general overview

The students

Our undergraduate students, seeking to teach in secondary schools, undertake a four-year BA/BSc honours degree with Qualified Teacher Status. Their main subject study is in physical education with a subsidiary subject chosen from English, religious and moral education, geography and environmental science or information technology. Notionally the modular degree offers considerable flexibility with opportunities for a change of direction or career destination during the first two years. The course is very popular, however, and applications are overwhelming. Admission procedure is rigorous and, in addition to a sound academic background and high sporting profile, applicants are expected to demonstrate a commitment to secondary teaching so that, once established within the course, they are unlikely to deviate from a clear professional route. A typical undergraduate will be fresh from a sixth form having achieved solid GCSE passes and sound grades in, probably, three A levels. He (and despite a vigorous equal opportunities policy and some increasing exceptions, our students tend to be white, male, young and middle-class) or she will probably play a sport at county level. These young undergraduates begin the course with a refreshing enthusiasm for teaching and their responsiveness allows for a lively and pleasing academic interaction.

The Educational Studies course

Our two-year programme of Educational Studies is taught during the third and fourth years of the degree course and is part of a wider professional pathway which includes subject application work in both main and subsidiary areas and which combines school-based with college-based elements so that students are able to both prepare for and reflect upon their teaching practice. A modular '2 + 2' degree dictates that, although students are involved in periodic school experience during the first two years of their course, the initial emphasis is upon subject study, and it is not until their third year that they undertake a block teaching practice.

During the first semester of this third year, students make a series of preliminary visits to their teaching practice school in order to familiarise themselves with procedures and organisation, to meet staff and to arrange a suitable timetable. They then undertake a five-week practice which is essentially diagnostic in that strengths and weaknesses are identified and acted upon, which will provide experience and material for their subsequent work in college. At the beginning of the second semester they return to the same school to undertake their second five-week practice which is then summatively assessed against clearly specified competence criteria. It is around this 'double-centred' teaching experience that our Educational Studies programme is developed in its first two-semester year. In Semester 1 attention is given initially to preparation for teaching practice and, later, to reflection upon the experience with an emphasis upon the classroom context. Throughout this period, and in addition to a teaching practice file, students are asked to maintain an observation diary and, for their assessed assignment, to present a school experience journal.

Much the same pattern is followed during Semester 2 with the emphasis now placed upon the wider forms of school organisation which support effective teaching and learning. At this stage seminars become more formalised and students must give timed and fully prepared presentations to their peers as assessment tasks complementary to a written assignment.

During the fourth and final year of their studies students are involved in school-based research in pursuit of their own supervised project which is presented as a 'long-study'. In their final semester and prior to their final six-week block practice, their work in Educational Studies examines schools within a wider social context.

Year 3 – the professional pathway: the first semester

Within this necessarily very brief sketch of a two-year undergraduate programme, we wish to give attention to our work with students in the first semester and would highlight particular features:

- As participants in lectures and seminars and in presenting their work, students are involved in a planned variety of both written and spoken communication.

- In undertaking Educational Studies, students are required to work collaboratively and to outline their ideas to others succinctly and cogently.

- Their study includes both directed and independent research within the relevant academic literature; the scrutiny of school-based resources and materials; properly conducted classroom enquiry and observation, albeit on a small scale.

Practice, then, is central to this programme but theory is not neglected. Rather, we attempt to make theoretical assumptions explicit; we aim to provide students with opportunities to discuss theory and, importantly, to tease out the values and ideologies with which it is entwined. This, of course, has the potential to be dull stuff indeed, and certainly we remember many of the Education lectures associated with our own training with something less than pleasure.

Yet the programme succeeds. Educational Studies sessions are lively and characterised by activities, discussions and presentations. There are, certainly, taught elements but, essentially, we would point to two key aspects:

● the course is rooted in the meaningful context of students' immediate teaching experience

● the sessions take place within conditions of psychological safety – a learning environment where students can operate with some sense of ease and security.

This is not, then, a denial of theory for that would be an intellectual dishonesty. Theory is always present and needs to be made explicit; to offer merely practice is simply to offer the aridity of more of the same – experience without concomitant understanding. This is not, however, theory 'jammed into the brain'. The metaphor is a crude version of teaching by transmission and offends our more complex understanding of how learning best takes place. Theory, rather, needs to be related to experience, to be given meaning, to be enlivened with a grounding in experience.

We shall now attempt to illustrate our work by drawing upon two complementary and contiguous elements from the Educational Studies programme in the first semester 'Communication in the Classroom' and 'Making Sense of Classrooms', both of which provide sessions before and after students' first teaching practice.

Methodology

How do we convey the dynamic of what, as mere paper description, may seem fairly pedestrian practice? Here we echo Groundwater-Smith.

> How can writers of educational experience ... set out in an engaging narrative form what may often seem humdrum, even trivial, so that the reader can discover for himself or herself more profound insights into educational processes?
> (Groundwater-Smith 1984, p.5)

In framing her answer, Groundwater-Smith draws attention to the 'potency' of 'non-literary fiction', to the 'new' journalism and the 'story as photograph'. We would build on this by offering a case study approach which, within a naturalistic paradigm, offers opportunity for illuminative evaluation achieved through what Stake (1977), refers to as 'portrayal'. Such an approach which 'should be helping people keep in touch with the reality of instruction' is, in our view, necessarily selective. 'If,' claims Stake, 'the programme glows, the evaluation should reflect some of it. If the programme wobbles, the tremor should pass through the evaluation report' (Stake 1977, p.162).

In attempting, then, to convey something of the texture of our work with students it is what we detect as the 'glows' and 'wobbles' to which we shall mainly direct attention.

The video camera and tape recorder have become very much a part of our naturalistic research approach to which students themselves have grown accustomed – often operating the equipment themselves and always keen to view and comment upon the recordings made. Involved as we are in the lives, work and aspirations of these students – many are our personal tutees; we supervise many of them on teaching practice and conduct individual tutorials – we feel at ease in our frequent professional interactions and would claim our research stance to be ethnographic. Much of our data take the form of description and transcription. Acknowledging that what we offer is not events themselves but interpretations of those events we feel, nonetheless, that our research is conducted in a participatory manner and that our data are presented in a form which allows the possibility of a variety of interpretation. Further, in describing our work, it is not our intention to boast a model of good practice but, rather, to investigate what, intuitively, seems good practice. It is, too, an enquiry into our own work in ITE and a declaration of underpinning values; it is a determination to learn and, subsequently, to improve the quality of our own teaching and learning.

Making sense of classrooms

Getting organised

Particularly during the first semester of their third year and immediately prior to their first teaching practice, students are obviously concerned with the immediacies of classroom management. 'Will I be able to keep control?' is the common if sometimes invoiced question. The first 'lectures' in Educational Studies at this stage have three complementary purposes:

1. to alert students to those immediate strategies of classroom organisation and communication which help to establish 'ground rules'

2. to indicate a clear relationship between orderly classroom management, clear aims and detailed planning and preparation

3. to suggest how observations and reflections can be recorded in ways which allow a school experience journal to be maintained and, later, presented for assessment.

Informed reflection is the key to our work here as this, after all, will not be a 'deep end' experience for students. As was suggested earlier, all will have taken part in serial school experience programmes related to their main subject studies during Years 1 and 2; preparatory work for teaching practice is also simultaneously undertaken in main and subsidiary subject application sessions; students, anyway, will have made preliminary visits to their teaching practice schools and, during their first week of teaching, will be involved in participant observation. Such nurturing is designed not to mollycoddle students, the majority of whom are robust young practitioners with clear teaching potential, but to provide space and structured opportunities for observation, reflection and discussion so that they will begin to develop an informed understanding of the profession in which they are now involved.

Following some introductory 'orientation' lectures relating to the National Curriculum and recent developments in secondary schooling, the Educational Studies programme involves students in an understanding of the principles of good practice demonstrated through role-play and through response to video-taped examples of teachers at work. Attention is drawn, for example, to the use of voice and gesture; to the way in which a teacher might position him/herself in the classroom, his/her mobility and eye-contact. Student volunteers enact similar teaching roles with their peers in which they practise some basic control strategies. Students, in groups, prepare and present elementary 'ground rules' for classroom behaviour to their colleagues.

Remarkable to us is the apparent and innocent lack of urgent preparatory awareness amongst students regarding, for example, punctuality, the preparation of books, materials, board work and general classroom arrangements. Here we are tempted to divert in order to speculate regarding the kinds of responsibility extended to school pupils for their own lives and learning. Is it fair to claim that their experience of schooling has been so structured that they believe, faintly, in the miracle of things just happening? And lecturers are not above a little deception in demonstrating these concerns. In a module which repeatedly draws the attention of students to professional concerns and protocol, there is surprise on the morning of the fourth session in the second week to find the module leader, Tom Sweeney, absent, and the room disorganised. The students begin hesitantly to prepare the room in its usual pattern of grouped chairs and tables, and Tom enters hurriedly, flustered and late. Normally given to informal preamble he now turns his back on the assembled students and busies himself with the overhead projector and his transparencies. He begins the lecture abruptly, in 'delivery' style, with no apology for his lateness and with no contextual information but, in mid-flow, is interrupted by a student arriving late. Given a hard stare by Tom, the student sits, the lecture resumes only to be interrupted minutes later by another late-comer whom, this time, Tom rounds on and scolds for the impertinence of being late. A few moments later Tom stops his lecture again to ask with irritation if a student is talking and to point out that he is not taking notes. The student becomes a little bullish in defence − he was only asking to borrow a pen from a colleague − using some mild backchat. The atmosphere, by now, is tense: the scene seems set for an altercation. Embarrassed students, quite unused to such tension within the context of HE, sink bemused into the insubstantial refuge of their seats. What is happening here, and might they be 'picked on' next? But then Tom stops, smiles, and tells them to relax. They have, of course, been the victims of an innocent subterfuge between the lecturer and some selected students designed to demonstrate the relationship between classroom management and personal and professional organisation. The subsequent relief allows a sound basis for shared discussion of productive organisational strategies.

Students, of course, are aware that, in the hurly-burly of classrooms, they will have to think rapidly and on their feet. Here, at least, they have the opportunity to simulate something of that thinking, and from these early lectures arises a basic procedural model for orderly classroom management.

Similarly, in a preparatory session on 'Communication in the Classroom', students work from an experiential base − an exchange of experience with regard to language variation – to consider a model of communication. This is enlivened through the use of video – watching both pupils and teachers at work – and through group activity designed to draw the attention of students to the enormous range of communicative competence demonstrated by teachers. In addition to obvious aspects of classroom communication this range includes: body language; the 'scaffolding' language used to support learning; an understanding of the relationship between language use and personal and social identity; the bureaucratic language, mostly written, in which teachers are increasingly involved; and the communicative skills needed within committee work. Rather than imposed, however, this model of communication is constructed through student discussion, a sharing of 'language autobiographies' and an audit of perceived personal communicative strengths and weaknesses. Students faced, too, with a need to use observation notes as a basis for an academic essay are provided with a view of those purposeful communicative strategies, like drafting and evaluation, which characterise much language use in school.

This brief overview of some preliminary and pre-teaching practice features of our course is intended to indicate the substantial ground of practice in which our theoretical work will be rooted. Essentially we begin not only with students' experience but also the anticipation of that experience.

This, we feel, can be usefully illustrated in more detail through selected transcriptions from a single session – 'Making Sense of Classrooms' – where students, newly returned from their first teaching practice, revisit those issues of management, communication and control which were the topics of their earlier lectures.

Student voices and commentary

The thirty-four students are seated in self-selected groups of fives and sixes around tables in a spacious teaching room equipped with video facilities and overhead projector. The session is taught by Tom Sweeney and is being recorded on video by Robert Catt. The informality is immediately striking. Many of the students, if not 'untidy', have certainly dressed down for the session, and the many track suits, trainers and baseball caps in evidence are a marked indicator that the first teaching practice has been completed. Many students have not seen each other for some weeks, and there is a buzz of gossip, jokes, anecdote and informal evaluation: 'How did you get on?' 'Great. No probs. Terrific department. Kids were smashing' etc., although, and thankfully less frequently, 'It was a nightmare!' is heard.

In his introduction, Tom Sweeney gives attention to the topic of classroom management, particularly in relation to what Brown and McIntyre (1993, p.54) characterise as the Normal Desirable State (NDS) of classroom behaviour. This problematic and value-laden formulation is treated, at this stage, unproblematically and uncritically and as a convenient shorthand for those orderly conditions to which students understandably aspire.

A structured evaluation of the first teaching practice then takes place with students working first in groups and then in pairs. General comments are subsequently invited and, briefly prior to the point at which the transcription begins, comparisons have been made between the management and characteristic behaviour of different age groups.

As students talk an immediate atmosphere of release and safety is apparent. Students speak, often quickly, with some conspiratorial excitement as they swop experiences. And this is supportive, rather than challenging, discussion: momentarily free of the encumbering apparatus of performance criteria and the formality of assessment – albeit diagnostic – they are keen to listen and contribute to the immediately personal testimony of others who, like them, have at last 'been there'. A swopping of stories, certainly, but that narrative exchange is skilfully supported by a college lecturer who, reflecting-in-action, provides those nuances of guidance which provide direction towards the satisfaction of a final goal.

Unsurprisingly, the difficulty of managing Year 9 groups emerges as a theme, and this is picked up by Keith who speaks quickly and fluently eliciting much sympathetic laughter from the group.[1]

Keith: Year 10s and Year 11s were more rewarding because you had to work harder with them . . . you could actually see results . . . whereas with a lot of the younger kids . . . especially Year 7 you had to realise that some of them had just come out of junior school . . . and . . . some groups I wouldn't have a problem with but others . . . there'd be

1. A note on transcription: pauses are simply indicated by an ellipsis ('...'); contextual comment is inside square brackets, for example [*laughter*] and overlap is written with the two lines of speech bracketed together ("{') on adjacent lines. Indented speech indicates an absence of gap between turns, indicative in itself of the speed, excitement and shared purpose in the discussion. A commentary follows each transcribed passage.

kids that'd want to get up out their seats every other second
and run around the classrooms and grab a pen, a pencil,
go and get a sharpener [*group laughter*] and ... well, they
didn't ... they weren't used to having to sit down in their
seats ... [*group laughter*] and they kept on ... sticking
their hands up to ask questions. They'd been encouraged
to ask questions through their junior school ... so ...
to have that ... I had one class like that in Year 7 ...
that when I actually looked at their books ... and what
they actually got through in the lesson ... they ... they
really [*he laughs*] didn't do much [*group laughter*] I just
spent ... a lot of time really getting them to sit down,
to stop asking questions and really trying to get things
over to them ... Whereas I had the same subject and
the same subject area with a Year 8 ... that were used
to sitting down and were so much better disciplined ...
and ... they got through about four times the amount of
work. So it was more rewarding having the Year 8 than
the Year 7 {that ...

Tom: {Let me just for a moment go back to that ...
that general sort of nod and murmur of ... of ... of
agreement on Year 9 ... in between there where somebody
said cockiness and ... and everything that ... Can
some ... can people just sort of, er, amplify that a bit
more ...? What do we actually mean by cocky? What
were some of the actual, if you like, NDS sort of normal
desirable or undesirable states of pupil activity, with Year
9s ...? What were they actually doing which made them
cocky?

Commentary

Here we have something of a 'wobble'. Keith's monologue clearly
has much potential for further discussion, throwing up as it does
some immediate concerns. We meet again a metaphor of learning
as transmission 'trying to get things over to them' – and a concomitant denigration of pupil activity – 'getting them to sit down
to stop asking questions'; there is a view of classroom activity as
production – 'when I actually looked at their books ... they really
didn't do much ... Year 8 got through about four times the amount
of work'; there is a stereotypical belief that the classroom style of the
primary school 'there'd be kids that'd want to get up out of their

seats every other second ...' – is incompatible with that of the secondary school and is, anyway, soon eradicated – 'Year 8 were used to sitting down and were so much better disciplined'.

Tom's strategy is to cut into Keith's monologue at the point where redundancy begins and to push discussion on. Here there is a teaching dilemma and, I suggest, in Tom's syntactical repairs as he interrupts Keith is evidence of a temptation to react to a seeming mountain of pedagogical prejudice. But this is resisted. Conversation analysts point to the principles of co-operation and co-ordination which facilitate communication. Tom is building on these here, and to have challenged Keith would have been to sabotage the listening and facilitating role Tom has adopted. Reflection-in-action is evident in Tom's tentative response, and it is worth noting that he echoes Keith's repeated use of 'actually'. Is Keith, albeit implicitly, drawing attention to the experiential, the reality, the authenticity of informed opinion, viz. I know this because I was there/did this? Tom's 'What were they actually doing?' draws students back to their discursive task. Gary, however, taking up the discussion now fumbles for an explanation rooted in adolescent psychology which also 'wobbles'. Tom, aiming to highlight the immediacy – the practicality – of experience, seizes upon that use of 'testing' to initiate two further lively contributions:

Gary: ... they grow up a little bit more and realise they don't have to act like kids all the time. They're trying to act older ... want to be treated a lot older ... so you have that transition period in Year 9 where they're not sure whether they're young or that ... not sure whether they're old, um ... and they sort of act most strangely out ... quite out of character and are sort of ... big handful. They're testing you to see how far they can get in ... um ... get away with it ... um ... and other times they'll be very wary of you {so ...

Tom: {Give me some examples from some others of this testing that goes on. What were they actually ... what would you ... classify as a test to you? What sorts of things do they do?

Brian: I just thought of, I had one lad ... um ... Annemarie had him in a rugby group actually {which was a ...

Annemarie: {I know him. [laughing] Yeah.

Brian: And ... um ... er because my name's Mr Ford he sort of
           answered me ... found out ... my name's Mr Ford ...
           'Well, where's the Sierra?' And every ... [*laughing*] single
           lesson ... [*laughing; loud group laughter*] every single
           lesson ...[*louder group laughter*] he said, 'Where's
           the Sierra?' It was impossible to answer ...I had him
           for ... [*laughing*] What sort of ... [*unintelligible*] ...
           Mr Ford ... a running joke [*long passage of loud group
           laughter*] And sometimes you [*group laughter*] can take it
           as funny ... At other times you [*group laughter fading*]
           can ... The way ... the way he said it was downright
           offensive. [*group laughter*]

Tom: All right. All right ... That's ... that's ... that's ...
           what I mean. David you've had your hand up. What
           sort ...? How were you tested by {Year 9 ...?

David: {I was ... There's a
           lad I had for a health and fitness lesson and he was very
           outgoing thing ... you know ... sort of ... There was a
           CCF [*combined cadet force*] at the school and he was, er,
           always walking round with this army gear ... so I ... in
           this lesson we were doing, like a fitness thing, I ... as a
           joke to sort of ... get on with him ... I sort of talked to
           him like a sergeant major. So I sort of went, 'Get down and
           give me thirty press ups.' And he went ... [*group laughter*]
           he's looking at me and he went ... I thought, all right
           forget this, it's not working ... And then a bit later I
           was walking across the yard at break time, he come up
           to me and he punched me in the arm ... I turned round.
           I looked down at him and he went [*mimics*], 'Come on
           sir, me and you now' ... [*extended loud group laughter*]
           [*unintelligible*] ... walking on. He pulled my arm again,
           looked at me, said [*mimics*], 'Sir, if I had a fight with you,
           it'd be three hits: me hit ... [*loud group laughter*] hitting
           you, you hitting the floor and the ambulance hitting ninety'
           [*prolonged group laughter*]. {So I ...

Student 2:   {I haven't heard the last one
           before ...

David: ... said, 'Come up when you're a bit bigger' ... Well
           and then I just walked off ... I mean he stood there
           shouting at me but ... I just ignored him. [*loud sympa-
           thetic laughter*]

Tom: Great ... I think that's a superb example of a test, er ... was that Year 9 as well?

David: Yeah, Year 9.

Tom: Year 9. [*group laughter fading*]

Commentary

Student 2 is clearly drawn into the excitement of sharing David's anecdote in a very public way. The video and tape recordings of the narration also reveal facial gesture and excited intonation suggesting how important this incident has been for David. As a young male PE student he is aware of his susceptibility to physical challenge which, here, he tries to play down with a forced insouciance, 'I just walked off,' and by giving attention to the idiosyncratic story of the three hits. Like Brian, he is perplexed by the difficult situation in which he finds himself, and he shares that uncertainty about how 'to take it'. Both examples point to the need for further reflection – the need not only to share but to make sense of and understand the experience. Brian makes an appeal to a colleague to support the nature of his difficulty. The corroborative, 'I know him. Yeah,' is the kind of prop which Sylvia – in the following transcript – also receives ('he was always like that'). There is an embryonic collegiality here required by us all to separate the personal and sometimes painful experience from the more appropriately professional.

Sylvia who speaks rapidly, almost breathlessly, is clearly pleased to tell her story.

Tom: Anybody else as well ...? Sylvia?

Sylvia: I had a Year 9 guy come up to me after my gymnastics lesson and turn round and say, 'Miss I know more about gymnastics than you do ...' But he was like really he was ... really cocky the whole time. When I spoke to his ... what would be ... his normal teacher afterwards ... she said that he was always like that. So I didn't feel so bad about it. But when he spoke to me first I felt, well, terribly inadequate as a teacher and as a teacher of gymnastics. I thought, good God, give me a few years more. I just turned round to him, [*changes to assertive tone*] 'Well, I've had three years' experience of gymnastics. Have you had that long?' Made out in front of all these people all this experience I'd had ... [*sympathetic group laughter*]

Commentary

Within a supportive environment, Sylvia is able to speak openly about what could have been a damaging criticism from a pupil. Students, pleased with completed lessons will often report that pupils declared, 'That was a good lesson, Miss', 'I enjoyed that' etc. Negative comments can be hurtful and Sylvia admits to feeling 'terribly inadequate as a teacher'. Interestingly, in his criticism of the teacher's subject knowledge, the pupil finds something of an Achilles' Heel amongst students. In our experience subject knowledge is a perceived vulnerability, and here the student adopts two strategies: she takes some comfort from a colleague's reassurance that the pupil 'was always like that', and, apparently, she bluffs her way through 'in front of these people all this experience I'd had'.

Tom now moves tentatively towards closure.

Tom: Good ... good. All right ... right. Any other commonalities? We ... we've got to finish in a couple of minutes but are there any other sort of themes coming through? Year 9 is an obvious theme ... coming through ... Anything else ...?

Keith: A commonality was when I ... if you had a difficult group, right? But myself and a few other people ... the way we got ... through to them is actually not ... not just seeing them once a week but actually taking some of your free time and getting involved with them in another area, whether it's finding other lessons of PE or games on the curriculum or even if they're getting involved in the out ... out-of-school clubs ... where they actually see them as pupils ... And you wouldn't actually be taking the club but you'd get involved with the club and they'd see you without you having to be like a disciplinarian with them ...

Tom: That's right ...

Keith: ... so they {have to ...

Tom: {The pressure is off you in a way there. If it's somebody *else's* lesson you're helping out with or a club, the pressure's off in terms of ... having to get through work, isn't it? Or having to discipline the whole class or something.

Keith: Right.

Tom: And did that? You did that and ... {that ...

Keith: {Yeah.

Tom: ...worked?

Keith: Yeah. Worked with a couple of classes.

Commentary

Here Keith, perhaps sensing Tom's move towards a conclusion, moves the discussion on by picking up 'commonalities' and – demonstrating a pedagogical awareness seemingly absent from his earlier contribution – makes a significant point regarding a shared approach to a problem – 'myself and a few other people' – which results in a positive strategy. 'Getting involved in the out-of-school clubs' provides a possibility for action. There is, he seems to suggest, something which students can do to overcome a general problem. The point, perhaps, is still a little particular but Tom moves to support the student by indicating the value of such an approach – 'the pressure's off'. With apt felicity Reg now pushes towards the need for such support to be organised rather than left to chance.

Reg: We had that at my school anyway where it was organised. Our lessons were ... my lessons were organised, um, in that ... I took say a group, um ... I had two groups for English ... I took them for gymnastics as well and, um, we also had specific lessons in which we were just observing and helping out ... so that they'd see us but we weren't the main sort of teacher but we'd be helping out advising you know ... one-to-one if there was someone really weak or whatever. So in that sense it was set up for us ... as assistants ... It was really good for us.

Tom: I think we'll have to leave it there because we'll be able to come back to some other points on Thursday ... when Robert leads the session ... But, er ... I hope it's for ... for those of you who are now beginning to get stuck into the writing ...of your assignments ... I hope the session

> in some ways was able to help with that ... But more
> importantly ... perhaps begins to show us ... all of us,
> really, that the idea of learning from experience is not just
> straightforward, it actually doesn't just happen ... One
> actually has to come away and think about it quite care-
> fully if we are actually ... er, to learn and benefit from
> it ... erm, an ... and hopefully as you will on your ...
> your next practice ... which won't be too far away.

Superficially pedestrian, the transcripts perhaps portray little of the significance of the rich exchanges which the session has fostered. Tom's point that 'learning from experience is not just straight-forward, it actually doesn't just happen' neatly sums up the introductory theme of the course which demands the interrogation of and reflection upon experience. Not in itself an innovative point, it has, however, been made – albeit indirectly – by the students themselves. The seemingly conversational 'scaffolding' structure of the introductory course, and this evaluation session in particular, has allowed students to make their own way to a pertinent con-clusion. Such student reflections upon practice, we would claim, exemplify the value of 'grounded theory' and the importance of socially constructed and conversationally shared awareness.

For those 'beginning to get stuck into the writing' there is now a clear indication of intended direction. Robert Catt, in his guidance on student approaches to writing has already pointed out that the school experience journal has the status of the academic essay and must draw upon recommended reading and seminars as well as observed and participatory experience. He has been given a cue here by Tom which will facilitate a 'way in' to the subsequent and preparatory writing session.

Of related interest here is a brief extract from David's journal dealing with his disturbing Year 9 incident:

> Although the school was traditionally interested in rugby the Year Nine pupils appeared to have a distinct dislike to it. This made my job very difficult as it was hard to show that rugby was a fun game to pupils who had already decided it wasn't. Year Nine in particular was a very difficult year to teach as a lot of them appeared to have a chip on their shoulders deeming the lessons to be 'pointless!' I felt that there was a personality clash between a number of boys in the class and never really felt that I had a good rapport with them. The worst incident occurred during my last week of teaching practice during a Year Nine Health and Fitness class which I actually found enjoyable to teach. The boys had to complete a fitness circuit

working at each station for four minutes and then taking their pulse. In the class there was one particular boy who was interested in the army yet he was showing no inclination to work. I turned to him mimicking a sergeant major and jokingly told him to 'get down and give me 30'. I thought that a bit of humour would do the trick but unfortunately it was taken the wrong way as he thought I was ridiculing him. The following day while I was walking through the yard I felt a hand on my shoulder and turned to see the same pupil taunting me 'come on sir'. He continued to try to start a fight telling me that, 'come on sir, me and you, if me and you had a fight there would be three hits! Me hitting you, you hitting the floor and the ambulance hitting 90!' I laughed at him and told him to return when he was a little bigger and proceeded to walk off. At the time I treated the incident as a joke but looking back on the situation I think it was definitely more serious than that.

David's well received narrative has obviously allowed him to shape the incident in his writing. There is now an uncomfortable and stiff formality to the piece 'deeming the lessons', 'proceeded to walk off' redolent of an 'incident' report. Of significance, however, is the shift of mood away from the earlier shared hilarity resulting from some obvious reflective attention: 'At the time I treated the incident as a joke but looking back on the situation I think it was definitely more serious than that.'

Educational Studies as practical knowledge

What, then, might be drawn from the tentative discourse of such novice teachers? At least, we would claim, there is an emergence of what Schön (1987, p.26), characterises as 'reflection-on-action'. That is, student teachers are encouraged to reflect on events from their own teaching and to generate questions, possibilities and insights from their practice as they are involved in it. They begin to theorise or problematise the situation in a manner to which Munby and Russell in an essay review of Schön's work draw our attention:

Seeing a professional puzzle differently becomes the essence of reflection in action, and is the foundation of the form of practical knowledge that, Schön argues, is so different from technical rationality.
(Munby and Russell 1989, p.77)

That ability to see teaching as a practical activity that is essentially problematic is a distinguishing characteristic of the 'reflective practitioner'. Practice is at the heart of this enterprise and, as we have indicated, the focus of our Educational Studies programme will shift from observation of experienced teachers to simulated experience to the students' own classroom encounters. Further, the Professional Pathway supports corresponding shifts between college and school, and between the 'real' and the simulated. The design of the course allows theoretical connections to form out of an understanding of practice and, as indicated, we have tried to provide students with a framework for making sense of those quotidian dilemmas of management and organisation which they will meet in school. A consequent emphasis upon appropriate presentation makes demands upon students to participate, prepare and evaluate their contributions in a safe and supportive environment where 'good practice' can be both discussed and modelled. And in constructing such a supportive framework we are drawing upon our own considerable experience and knowledge.

A particular influence upon the design of this framework is that of reflection as 'Critical Inquiry' (Adler 1991). Initially, we recognise the need to support students with a broadly technical approach to classroom management and organisation related to basic principles of good practice. Yet a set of rules cannot account for all circumstances and, in what Schön calls the 'swampy lowlands' of schools, students will have to confront 'messy, confusing problems' that 'defy technical solution' (Schön 1987, p.3). Classrooms are untidy places, and students who are unable to inquire into their own practice will quickly rely routinely on strategies that may or may not be the most appropriate.

As they proceed along the Pathway it is expected that students will develop their practical knowledge, that is 'thinking on one's feet', together with more deliberative reflection. To do this they need to give due regard to historical, social and institutional contexts: they need also to understand that the management structure of schools is complex and dynamic. Schools' organisational procedures – and the values and beliefs which inform them – are markedly different and not always conducive to reflection. The opportunity for comparison of experience within a supportive environment as has been briefly indicated here is designed to provide students with an opportunity to move beyond a concern with particular versions of classroom experience and to introduce them to that critical disposition of mind which will enable them to both cope with and move beyond immediate professional concerns.

While recognising the limitations of such a brief sketch of aspects of our current work we hope, nonetheless, to have illuminated the unpleasant crudity of that 'theoretical' caricature designed to denigrate the work of teacher educators.

References

Adler, S. (1991) 'The reflective practitioner and the curriculum of teacher education', *Journal of Education for Teaching*, **17** (2), pp.139–50.
Brown, S. and McIntyre, D. (1993) *Making sense of teaching*. Buckingham: Open University Press.
Groundwater-Smith, S. (1984) 'The portrayal of schooling and the literature of fact', *Curriculum Perspectives*, **4** (2), pp.1–6.
Munby, H. and Russell, T. (1989) 'Educating the reflective teacher', *Journal of Curriculum Studies*, **21** (1), pp.71–80.
Schön, D.A. (1987) *Educating the reflective practitioner*. London: Jossey Bass.
Stake, R. (1977) 'Description versus analysis', in Hamilton, D., Jenkins, D., King, C., MacDonald, B. and Parlett, M. (Eds) (1977) *Beyond the numbers game*. London: Macmillan, pp.161–2.

CHAPTER 5

Music Today – and Tomorrow?

Christine Edwards

Outline of study

This is a case study of the HE tutor and her involvement in the music programme of a Creative Arts module for third year primary students in ITE specialising in Environmental Studies.

A visit by the students to a nearby primary school is the particular focus of this study. It will be used as an example of the benefits of HE-based work for student teachers. The relationship between HE, local schools and local authority advisory work and the role they might play in enhancing the quality of students' learning and experience will be discussed.

The question will be posed as to whether these resources and opportunities will be available in the future or could be provided by a school-centred training programme.

Introduction

The students in this study were specialising in environmental studies. As part of their professional studies they were involved in a Creative Arts programme covering art, drama and music. These three arts were taught as discrete subjects for the first four weeks of the module. For the last three weeks the students worked in groups on a collaborative project, producing a short production which they presented to an audience of Year 3 children from a nearby school.

In these students' previous music sessions at the beginning of their second year my priority was to develop their musical self-esteem and involve them in music making at a level at which they felt comfortable. An important part of any music programme in initial training is best done in a supportive group where there are opportunities for experiment and discovery, trial and error.

Many students when they arrive in college will have had no practical music experience since the age of fourteen and it may have left them with negative perceptions of the subject and of their own musical competence. An enquiry into the arts in primary initial training (Cleave and Sharp, 1986) revealed widespread lack of confidence in this curriculum area among students entering college. If they have lacked opportunities to play classroom instruments or keyboards, they will need to go through the same process of experimentation and skills development, albeit at their own level, as the young pupils they will meet in schools. The processes will to some extent mirror children's own musical progress and offer valuable insights into the nature of learning in music.

In the students' third year, alongside practical sessions – trying out songs, games and activities to take on their final teaching practice – it was necessary to develop their observational skills. Listening and observing are central to work in the classroom. Glover and Ward (1993), suggest that the ability to monitor children's musical behaviour, and provide experiences to match abilities and develop them, is more important in a teacher than performing skills. This observational and diagnostic approach is taken for granted in other subject areas but needs to be encouraged and developed in music sessions with students. Many teachers involved with music education in schools, as Jo Glover comments:

> still have little background history or 'habit' of observing children's music making in a way that allows entering into or assessing their musical understanding.
> (Glover 1990, p.257)

As she points out, teachers understand children's mathematical development because they have considerable practice at it. Opportunities for students to observe children's music making in the classroom are limited by the constraints of time and finding nearby schools with lively curriculum music and teachers prepared to accommodate them. It was important that the third year students had this experience.

By negotiating timetabling with colleagues I was able to take the students into a school for a whole afternoon to observe music at Key Stages 1 and 2 and work with small groups of Year 5 children. It is this school visit which became the main focus of my study as it encapsulated some of the issues currently under discussion concerning the future of ITE.

Background to the study

I started my teaching career as a music specialist in secondary and then primary schools. I later became a generalist primary teacher before moving in to a local authority advisory team as a music support teacher. For the last three years my time was equally divided between the LEA and working at the local HE college on the primary BA/QTS and PGCE courses. My joint appointment enabled me to share with the students curriculum materials which had been successfully piloted with pupils and teachers in LEA schools and to provide examples of good quality classroom practice for them to observe. As a relative newcomer to ITE I have continually reviewed my practice and work with students. While encouraging them to reflect on their teaching and become more self-critical, I also have had to adjust to my new role and rethink the way I work. I have used this very modest study as a useful exercise to reflect on the needs of students and the importance of HE to their education and support.

Having worked as it were on both sides of the educational fence I can acknowledge the debt I owe to colleagues in HE whose work has inspired and informed my own practice. With present uncertainty about the future of initial training, the importance of a continued role for HE in research and curriculum development will be discussed at the end of this chapter.

School visit

Outline of the lessons

As I indicated earlier, many students lack musical confidence. Few, it seemed, had initiated exploratory or creative projects in music on teaching practice. The music sessions in the third-year module were the last the students in this study would have on their ITE course, and they were anxious, with music now a foundation subject in the

National Curriculum, about their competence to teach it on their final teaching practice the following term. It seemed necessary to include a school visit in their programme to provide an opportunity to observe good classroom music making with time afterwards for discussion and reflection. I was able to take students to observe and participate in a music afternoon shared between myself and two class teachers in a local primary school in May 1993. The school had taken part in INSET programmes in the past. More recently, I had been working in an advisory capacity for the two previous terms with class teachers from Years 1–5. I spent five mornings a term in the school, leaving the teachers for the rest of the term to build on and extend the curriculum negotiated with them and initiated in the classroom sessions. The Year 5 teacher, while possessing no formal music skills, had benefited from LEA in-service development over several years and had become enthusiastic and confident enough to teach in front of groups of PGCE students earlier in the year. She had involved her class in improvising and composing, and introduced them to a wide range of music for listening, not only as part of their music programme but also to enrich work in other subject areas. The Year 2 class teacher had also very successfully followed up and extended the work started in the sessions I had shared with her. Both classes were examples of good practice and demonstrated the quality of work that could be expected from children of their age range and musical experience. This is important because many students will not necessarily have a real perception of standards and children's potential in music.

The outline and content of the lessons had been negotiated with the teachers, and introduced and discussed with the students, beforehand. Some of the songs and activities had been tried out in the college-based sessions and put in the context of children's musical development and the demands of the National Curriculum. These activities, engaged in with the peer group in college, were regarded with a healthy scepticism by a few of the students, judging by their body language and comments! By observing the children in these lessons, the students had the opportunity to evaluate the appropriateness of the activities and decide for themselves if they were enjoyable and motivated the pupils.

I taught the Year 2 class myself, assisted by the class teacher. As an experienced teacher with a very responsive class I was able to give the lesson pace and variety. I included songs, a musical game and a composing activity exploring long and short sounds, all of which the students had tried out themselves in college sessions. By starting with the early years and moving on to older children, I hoped to help students towards a better understanding of musical progression through Key Stages 1 and 2.

The Year 5 teacher led her class through a three-part round with actions, and through a Chinese song to which the class provided an accompaniment. This song, like most Chinese music, was in the pentatonic (five-note) scale. The children practised singing, playing and improvising in this scale. The class was organised into groups by their teacher to compose music using a poem as a stimulus, with opportunities for some of them to develop the pentatonic melodic patterns practised in the earlier part of the lesson. I took over at this point. I had introduced the poem the previous week and we had discussed its structure noticing the repeated verses and contrasting middle section. Working as a whole class the children had responded with ideas to re-create in music the mood and sounds suggested in the poem. I reminded them of the work we had covered in that lesson, and the children reproduced some of the ideas and tried out new ones. They then went away in their groups to create a short composition using the words as a framework and stimulus. A few children who received instrumental lessons used their violin, flute or guitar in a free way in their composition. The students each attached themselves to a group of children, sitting in to observe and giving help and encouragement when needed. Many of the children produced imaginative work and the afternoon ended with a brief discussion about the compositions among the teacher, children and students, providing opportunities for listening and appraising (Attainment Target (AT) 2 in the music National Curriculum document).

Observing and reflecting

The students stayed on to discuss the lessons they had observed. I asked them about the elements of pulse and rhythm in the Year 2 lesson. Referring to the song, 'Tony Chestnut', I pressed them to trace the development from the simple activity of keeping the actions to the beat to the more demanding task of omitting to sing on certain words until the whole song was performed in silence to the actions only – a way of encouraging the development of inner hearing. Did the majority of children perform this successfully without forgetting actions or speeding up? Were there any children with particular difficulties of co-ordination? Might they also be experiencing problems in other areas? The opening activity of 'Switch', a follow-my-leader game where the class copied rhythm patterns using different actions – clapping, patting knees, finger clicks and so on — was discussed. I pointed out the importance to many children of repetition before moving on to the next rhythm. Music cannot be held on the pause button. To extend the analogy with a tape recorder or video, the listener has to replay the music in his/her head and remember it. The circle format and the element of repetition give opportunities for the teacher to observe the children who picked up the new rhythm straight away and those who needed more time to absorb and reproduce it accurately. I stressed the importance of being able to stand back and observe, even in such a practical teacher-led lesson. Did I for instance sing with the class all the time? Were there moments where children shared a song, performed in small groups or on their own? Were there opportunities in the lessons for children to show that they were capable of more than either I or their teachers expected?

I introduced the concept of long and short sounds by blowing bubbles and encouraging the children to hum as the bubbles floated and make a short 'pop' sound when they burst. I told the students afterwards that I had not tried this idea out before with a class of children and was not sure whether it would work. As it happened, the class was responsive. I had built up a good rapport with them, and they and their teacher had obviously enjoyed the activity. I thought it important to show that I was prepared to take risks. We try in initial training to encourage students to be adventurous; not just to be content to play safe but push themselves forward in their planning and practice.

In the Year 5 class the students were impressed by the confidence of many of the children when improvising in the pentatonic scale, something they had found quite difficult when they had tried it themselves in the college session. The children's previous musical experience was discussed, and the students were able to deduce from the friendly and competent way they worked in groups that their teacher involved them on a regular basis in creative, collaborative learning. Many of the children were on their way to becoming independent learners in music — something that is difficult to achieve without giving them opportunities for individual and group work. Reflecting on their involvement with their assigned group for the composition work, the students were interested to see how surely some of the children found the sounds they wanted and fitted them together. When the students did intervene with a suggestion they commented wryly that it was frequently ignored. The experience gave them a brief insight into the delicate role of the teacher as facilitator and encourager in creative work in the arts and the fine line between imposing ideas and helping a group who are

84

struggling. The miracle of order emerging from chaos was also observed as a boisterous and unfocussed group of boys managed to produce something quite acceptable in the sharing at the end of the lesson.

Finally the students briefly considered extension activities and discussed which activities would have potential for cross-curricular links; learning in and through music which formed an important element in their Creative Arts module. I reminded them of a quotation from Janet Mills which I suggested should be in every student's head as they draw up a topic web: 'Cross-curriculum work is about enrichment not compromise' (Mills 1991, p.129).

Discussion and evaluation

The benefits of LEA links

One of the most important benefits of the music National Curriculum document is that it should help teachers to plan and present a more coherent music programme with a clearer understanding of development and progression than in the past. The students during this afternoon were presented with examples of Key Stages 1 and 2 work of a good (but in no way exceptional) standard, based on sound classroom practice by generalist teachers.

School-based work has become an increasingly important part of the students' programme, but, as I have already stressed, it is not always easy to find confident practitioners prepared to teach in front of or alongside students. This is where my work as an LEA advisory teacher was able to contribute to the range and quality of the HE music programme.

Over the years, through centrally and school-centred teacher in-service as well as work alongside colleagues in the classroom, I have been able to help schools improve their music provision and nurture and develop the confidence and effectiveness of individual teachers in their role as curriculum leaders. Relationships based on mutual trust and respect are not built up overnight and do not easily lend themselves to quality control and assessment by inspectors and administrators, as is the case in more high profile INSET programmes and workshops. I would suggest though that this long-term teacher development is invaluable not only to the schools and their pupils but also to the wider educational community including initial training.

Accommodation and resources

The quality of the school environment was an enhancing factor. The building was new and imaginatively designed with a large drama and music space as well as a central atrium which made group work with a class of thirty-five children a more aesthetically acceptable experience than the usual confinement within a single classroom. The school's own instruments were augmented by a variety of tuned and untuned instruments from college, including percussion from different musical cultures, so the children were not hindered by lack of resources.

I do not regard these details as trivial or peripheral. In ITE programmes we try to prepare students for the realities of school life and the challenge of providing interesting and stimulating work within the constraints of often inadequate buildings and resources. Music is an expensive subject to support, particularly now with the advent of music technology, and standards of provision in the subject can vary widely. Great stress is laid on the importance of students being given models of best practice to instil high standards and expectations. It should continue to be a concern in any future ITE programme.

The student perspective

From the student's perspective, the school visit was a useful part of the course, and it helped to set the work experienced in college into a classroom context. Unless they had been fortunate enough to have been involved in good classroom music while on teaching practice, this was their first planned school visit in music, and was obviously appreciated. In the students' evaluation of the module, comments included:

> It was good to see a music lesson with *children* – more of this.

> Particularly benefited from actually watching music lessons in school.

Most of the students felt that the Creative Arts module had increased their confidence through the practical 'hands on' approach of the lecturers. One student wrote:

Over the period of time I gained a lot of confidence and developed skills with encouragement and praise.

The students were very rewarding to teach. They came with a fresh and open attitude to the arts. They enjoyed the collaborative nature of the module with tutors and students working within and also across the arts. It is the aim of the course to send students into schools with a positive view of the arts and the enthusiasm to provide worthwhile learning experiences for their pupils.

The music sessions in ITE can take students only so far along the road to competency in directing and observing their pupils' musical learning. They will continue to need help and support with implementing the music curriculum. Some students may be fortunate enough in their first school to find a well planned music programme with a co-ordinator to help and advise. If not, to whom will they turn?

The perspective of the class teacher

The experienced and committed Year 5 teacher, Mrs A, kindly consented to an interview with me at the end of a typically busy day between a netball practice and a science INSET session. I am quoting verbatim from the recording of our meeting.

Mrs A did not regard herself as in any way a music specialist and had no formal music skills, but she considered her family background was a positive influence. Her father was a folk singer and taught her to play the penny whistle.

Mrs A's school was among those who volunteered to pilot the borough music project, teaching musicianship through singing, and she found the in-service development 'very, very useful'. She also had attended one of my 'World Music' courses and many of the songs and games she learned from it were still part of her classroom repertoire. An Orff Schulwerk course had introduced her to work in the pentatonic scale and the use of words and poetry in music education.

Both her headteacher and Mrs A were supportive of my efforts to provide opportunities for students to be involved in a classroom music lesson and were flexible over the timetable and made the students very welcome.

I questioned Mrs A about the afternoon with third year students and what she felt they might have gained from it. She underlined the importance of observing and being involved in a realistic classroom atmosphere – something different from working together in college. She stressed the importance of the quality of the encounter between lecturer and student:

> A lot of it is very personal I think ... it all depends on the actual individuals involved. The key thing is motivation and instilling confidence, I think. In any area of education if you've got someone to inspire you, you think, well I'll have a go and even if you fall flat on your face you pick yourself up and try again.

Mrs A had the special responsibility for supervising students on teaching practice and was involved in regular meetings with a linked HE college and other partnership schools. She had doubts about all schools being equally good at looking after and preparing student teachers based on her experience of helping students on teaching practice. There are in her opinion already problems in monitoring teaching practice in schools, and she is aware from students' comments that many do not receive the quality of support expected by the college.

> I am quite negative about the mentor schools. We are actually a mentor school. We take it quite seriously, but there are terrible discrepancies between schools. It really varies ... I don't see any easy answers to that ... There should be more monitoring both from the college and the school side on the actual students to see if they are going for the same aim which is to help someone on their way to QTS status.

Mrs A now has a music teacher working with her fortnightly, giving her a week in between to try out and develop ideas which she 'shows and shares' at the beginning of the following session. She is aware that a less confident colleague could feel intimidated. In her view it is important that the visiting teacher is seen as a supportive colleague and not an alienating 'expert'.

> I think the whole situation has got to be this support thing. It is team teaching, team learning.

LEA support and INSET courses are scarcer now and charge quite heavily for their services. Mrs A, like many teachers, is looking to the HE colleges to fill the gap. She is attending a twenty-day grant-related educational support for teachers (GEST) funded science course at my college and appreciates the opportunities to:

> meet other colleagues and make contacts from other boroughs ...
> A very good way of meeting and sharing ideas. I think maybe the
> HE colleges will take over the role of providing courses for working
> teachers. I think it is already happening now.

The perspective of the HE tutor

With the demands of the National Curriculum, greater emphasis on the core subjects and more time spent in schools, there is great pressure on the students. Now that music is a foundation subject in the National Curriculum, time has to be allocated for it in BA/QTS and PGCE courses. This is a positive benefit and should ensure a more even balance of provision and give the subject a higher status than has been the case in the past. Even so it is still doubtful whether it is possible to increase students' musical skills significantly, as well as covering the curriculum and children's musical development, without extra time and resources.

Because of their own very patchy music education, students often have no common model of exciting and structured music making on which to base their teaching and planning, unlike core subjects such as maths or English. Neither can they adequately read it up in a book. It was imperative that observation and involvement with children in schools should form part of this module. Standing back and reviewing the afternoon and my own involvement in it, I considered what had I learned and how I could improve the quality of the experience for future students.

A positive aspect for the students was the opportunity to observe a generalist teacher confidently sharing her skills and enthusiasm. In the lesson I taught in my role as specialist I avoided playing the piano. Such formal music skills are not essential for successful class teaching and can indeed hinder successful communication between teacher and pupil. Teaching a whole class lesson I was able to demonstrate the flow from one activity to the next with a variety of pace and mood that comes with experience.

The group composition was useful for allowing students to observe musical encounters but gave little opportunity to intervene as teachers. The performance at the end was appraised by teachers and children. The students were rather cast in the role of passive observers. Space should have been allowed for their contribution. As so often happens in school the bell rings and the valuable sharing of ideas is squeezed out because of the restraints of the timetable. Planning creative projects and allowing time for evaluation and discussion is a practical issue for students to consider when planning lessons on teaching practice. A video of the session would have allowed the students to look more closely at the pupils' musical behaviour. This would be a priority on another occasion.

The discussion with the students afterwards was a little constrained by their lack of experience in observing music making. They were perhaps unduly impressed by the Year 5 children; an indication of their limited experience of music in schools and low expectations in the subject. It has made me rethink some of my work with students. I am even more determined to find opportunities and strategies for developing their observation of musical processes and learning.

There is a misplaced perception that music is taught solely as a whole class activity. As Glover and Ward (1993) stress, opportunities for individual and group work are necessary to allow for development of skills and encouraging musical independence. As a follow-up to the school visit, the students might have benefited from planning such tasks, and trying them out and evaluating them in the classroom.

Concerns for the future

Implementing the music curriculum

Music was one of the last subjects to become a mandatory subject in the National Curriculum and like other arts subjects has, in the past, had to fight to maintain its place in the curriculum. Music educators have in recent years developed a coherent and compelling justification for the subject and its inclusion in the timetable. Keith Swanwick writing in 1994 describes the concerted efforts of professional musicians and teachers in 1992 to retain the *active* nature of music education in schools from the attempts by the National Curriculum Council (NCC) to introduce more theory and propositional knowledge into the curriculum. He writes:

> partly to fend off curriculum marginalisation and to find a compelling professional rationale, arts educators are always turning over and disputing the nature and value of their activity, trying to articulate a 'philosophy', attempting to define and defend their knowledge base; hence a readiness to respond to the challenge. (Swanwick 1994, p.60)

Having run the gauntlet of this professional lobbying, the then Secretary of State for Education, Kenneth Clarke, gave way and the two Attainment Targets were restored as 'performing and composing' and 'listening and appraising' (instead of 'knowledge and understanding').

There is a long tradition of pedagogy and research into instrumental and vocal techniques with numerous published treatises and instructional manuals. By contrast, music as a subject in schools available for all children has a more recent history. The role of HE has been crucial in the development of musical understanding, methodology and curriculum design. There has been a growth of interest in the newly emerging field of developmental and cognitive psychology of music which is increasing our knowledge of children's musical perception and learning. The research literature in music education is modest compared to other subject areas such as English and mathematics but it has been influential not only in the music National Curriculum document but has informed innovations such as the GCSE music syllabus, which has revolutionised secondary music programmes.

Despite fears in some quarters, music survived the Dearing Report's 'slimming down' of the National Curriculum. The document has been clarified and made more approachable for the generalist teacher, but no radical changes are anticipated. Whatever one's views of the National Curriculum the positive aspect is that schools can be expected to take the subject seriously and plan for progression and development in music. Everything would seem to be in place to ensure the entitlement of all children to a well planned music programme. Unfortunately as one door opens another closes. Local management of schools (LMS) and the weakening of local authority control have reduced centrally provided services. Curriculum support teachers are becoming an endangered species, and the work load of those remaining has reduced their effectiveness. It is particularly worrying that just as the teachers (especially general class teachers in the primary phase) most need their help and expertise, such support is no longer in place and the money for in-service development is directed into individual schools. Primary schools with their limited INSET budget have to buy in from the market-place or, if they still exist, into their own LEA courses which formerly were freely available. The Arts Council in a survey (Rogers 1993a) of LEA advisory and inspection services revealed that since 1988 almost two-thirds of LEA advisory teachers have gone, and with continual devolvement of budgets to schools the situation is unlikely to improve.

It is true that LEA services were not always targeted fairly. It could be said that schools keen to buy in help for music can still do so from freelance consultants, many of them formerly LEA advisers. Most headteachers, though, are working within tight financial constraints with conflicting priorities. HE, with its links with local schools, is needed more than ever to support the implementation of the National Curriculum.

Issues of quality

Music is now one of the subject areas receiving GEST funding. HE is eagerly planning and providing courses, filling the gap left by LEAs who may no longer have the staff or central resource areas to run their own. The twenty-day GEST-funded courses are particularly valuable in giving teachers time to develop skills and understanding.

There is an increasingly important role here for HE. The anxiety for the future is that as ITE becomes increasingly school-centred, there may not be HE departments left with the staff and resources to continue this work.

Primary teachers are in the main, flexible, imaginative and resourceful, but they are worried about their ability to implement the music curriculum. The Schools Curriculum and Assessment Authority (SCAA) has made great efforts to consult and listen to teachers and clarify the curriculum document. But in-service development is still needed to break down the fear of the subject; a fear often reinforced by musicians themselves. Music teachers have nurtured their specialist role and enjoyed ownership of craft skills like music notation, but have done little to encourage and value their colleagues' inherent knowledge – what Glover and Ward (1993, p.3), call 'competent adult' knowledge.

Teachers need encouragement to call on this basic competence to develop their skills in assessing and building up a musical profile of their pupils. The generalist practitioner is much better placed to monitor musical progress than a specialist colleague who sees the children only once a week. If they ignore music in their classroom teachers are sending negative signals about the status and value of the subject to pupils and parents.

Music is still regarded by some teachers, particularly in the later years of primary education, as a low-status subject and best left to the specialist. I also find these attitudes particularly among middle years students, and they surface in their course evaluations. A PGCE student commented:

> I personally feel music is a highly professional occupation and as such should be taught by a professional.

These perceptions are reinforced by experience on teaching practice when students are often positively discouraged from teaching music with their class because of pressure on the timetable and the existence of a visiting music teacher.

A report based on a series of seminars and conferences set up by the Arts Council (Rogers 1993a and 1993b) showed clearly that parents and governors are anxious to see music as an important part of school life. A recent enquiry into the initial implementation of the National Curriculum (Lawson, et al. 1994) found enthusiasm for music, but quoted two headteachers who expressed anxiety about the competitive educational climate which encourages Arts presentations as public relations exercises. The school concert, as a showcase involving a minority of children, is popular with parents and governors. There is not always the same concern and interest in ensuring good quality experiences for all pupils.

If school-centred initial training of teachers becomes the norm there will be concern about the standards and opportunities in arts subjects and music in particular. Schools may not be able to provide examples of good practice for students. Without some positive reinforcement from an HE programme, or monitoring and encouragement from curriculum leaders in schools, the new generation of teachers is unlikely to bring a change of attitudes. Unconfident students will become teachers who bring music-avoidance to a high art, leading in turn to another generation of students with poor musical self-esteem. Breaking this vicious circle is a challenge. If the position of music as a foundation subject in the National Curriculum is not just to become a cynical paper exercise, this chicken-and-egg cycle must be broken.

Developing the skills and confidence of students would pose problems for teacher-mentors. It is possible for students as well as teachers to pursue a musical journey alongside their pupils, developing confidence and musical understanding by improvising and composing with their pupils in the classroom. I'm sure this could be a valuable exercise and would help develop students' understanding of children's musical behaviour and development, but it is no substitute for a structured music programme and time for reflection away from the classroom. Would this learning alongside children be seriously considered adequate in maths or science?

Student teachers in HE departments do have the benefit of access to resources and curriculum materials of a greater variety than would be found in schools. Some students choose to do their special exercise in an aspect of music education and receive specialist tutorial support and access to a well-stocked library. On the present course at my college, working within a Creative Arts programme, students are helped towards an understanding of the distinctive contribution of the arts to a balanced education and the ways in which music can be developed in learning across the arts as well as a discrete subject. Written assignments help them to articulate and develop a theoretical basis for their work and, if they wish, to research in greater depth into the arts area in which they have a particular skill or interest.

It is important that HE continues to provide opportunities for creative work – composing individually or collaboratively. Swanwick and Taylor (1982) underline the importance of discovery for teachers as well as pupils and refer to Bruner's insistence that we should:

> enlist the natural energies that sustain spontaneous learning curiosity, a desire for competence, aspiration to emulate a model and a deep-sensed commitment to the web of social reciprocity.
> (Bruner 1966, p.127)

For students, making musical discoveries alongside their peer group is a means of engaging in this 'commitment to social reciprocity'. A well resourced HE department can offer these musical encounters within a context of trust and support provided by the tutor and the student group.

The collaborative nature of the course, and the way students help and support each other and share ideas and resources, is one of the most admirable features of college life. This supportive atmosphere is essential if students are to learn from their mistakes and grow in confidence and develop as self-critical and reflective practitioners. Betty Hanley, a lecturer at the University of Victoria, British Columbia, describes thus a music module in which students planned lessons, tried them out in local schools and assessed them back in college.

> The value of discussing plans and sharing special skills or backgrounds was evident in a number of lessons in which hidden talents

and resources surfaced. Further, it is clear that an important part of the learning was the feedback and evaluation given students. Breaking through natural resistance to constructive comments which are initially perceived to be criticism in the negative sense and moving to the student's assumption of the responsibility for self-assessment are of paramount importance if students are to take ownership of their learning. A collegial ambience is essential.
(Hanley 1993, p.14)

In the rush towards school-centred training this valuable aspect of college life should not be dismissed lightly. I would suggest that input from HE would still need to be an important element in any model of ITE. Swanwick and Paynter are critical of the move to school-centred initial training:

The teaching profession will begin to lose its cutting edge if systematically deprived of opportunities for critical reflection, self-evaluation and the extension of perspectives beyond the confine of one classroom.
(Swanwick and Paynter 1993, p.7)

The broadening of perspectives, curriculum initiatives, research into ways of understanding and assessing children's musical learning, have been led by college and university departments. From there they have filtered down and enriched work in the classroom. If government policy results in a weakening of HE how is this vital fertilisation of the curriculum to continue?

Curriculum development

The last two decades have seen an increase in curriculum initiatives and in the understanding of the musical learning and needs of children. The Inner London Education Authority (ILEA) invested heavily in music education, encouraging instrumental teaching in schools, resourcing classroom music generously and providing in-service development. Many of the best and brightest in music education were appointed as inspectors and co-ordinators in the 1970s and 1980s. In music as in many other areas ILEA led the country in curriculum ideas and materials, and many teachers like myself owe much to the support and inspiration we received from our ILEA colleagues.

Music support teams were established in many parts of the country, and developed curriculum materials and provided in-service development in their own areas. Universities produced innovative work in music technology, designing computer software and opening up new areas of musical exploration. In a more modest way, my own authority financed a vocally based music scheme for primary and special schools with songbooks and tapes including songs from the Indian subcontinent and other cross-cultural materials. My work with students is informed and supported by the methodology and curriculum materials which I helped to develop. The group who are the focus of this study were able to try out some of the songs and activities in college before observing them being used by teachers on the school visit. This is another example of the triangular relationship between HE, LEA and schools working to their common benefit. My colleagues and I were extremely fortunate to have been given time to trial materials and reflect on our work with teachers and find ways of improving their understanding of children's musical needs and progression. This experience helped to clarify my own thinking about music and gave me greater credibility and effectiveness in my HE role.

It seems unlikely that younger colleagues will have similar opportunities in the foreseeable future. Some authorities are valiantly keeping their support teams going but it will be increasingly difficult for them to find time and money for curriculum development. There are still able and experienced staff, many from ILEA and other authorities, who are using their energy and expertise to the benefit of HE. At the moment we are living on our musical capital. As these people move on and retire, and education departments in universities are threatened, we are left to face these important questions:

Where will the next generation of innovative, enthusiastic and inspiring music teachers come from?

We are spending our seed corn – are we considering the future harvest?

References

Bruner, J. (1966) *Toward a theory of instruction*. Harvard: Harvard University Press.

Cleave, S. and Sharp, C. (1986) *The arts: a preparation to teach*. London: NFER.

Glover, J. (1990) 'Understanding children's musical understanding', *British Journal of Music Education*, **7** (3), pp.257–62.

96

Glover, J. and Ward, S. (Eds) (1993) *Teaching music in the primary school*. London: Cassell.

Hanley, B. (1993) 'Music teacher education: new direct:ions', *British Journal of Music Education*, **10** (1), pp.9–21.

Lawson, D., Plummeridge, C. and Swanwick, K. (1994) 'Music and the National Curriculum in primary schools', *British Journal of Music Education*, **11** (1), pp.3–14.

Mills, J. (1991) *Music in the primary school*. Cambridge: Cambridge University Press.

Rogers, R. (1993a) *Looking over the edge: the survey*. London: Arts Council of Great Britain.

Rogers, R. (1993b) *Looking over the edge: the debate*. London: Arts Council of Great Britain.

Swanwick, K. (1994) *Musical knowledge*. London: Routledge.

Swanwick, K. and Taylor, D. (1982) *Discovering music*. London: Batsford.

Swanwick, K. and Paynter, J. (1993) 'Teacher education and music education: an editorial view', *British Journal of Music Education*. **10** (1), pp.3–8.

CHAPTER 6

Pin your Thoughts on the Wall: The Role of Display in the Classroom

Lynne Thorogood

Introduction

A primary focus of this chapter is the role of a tutor from an HE Education department in facilitating an understanding in students and teachers of the messages which can be transmitted to children through the school culture. Display has been chosen as the vehicle for the debate because it is so often under-utilised through being put up and arranged for the wrong reasons. Daniels points out that 'to have a nice bright classroom with lots of good display work is one of the commonly held indicators of good teaching practice' (Daniels 1989, p.124). It is not only students undertaking school placement who are concerned to enhance the appearance of their classrooms in order to create a good impression. An overheard conversation between two teachers concerning the promotion to headship of one of their colleagues concluded, rather caustically, 'I always knew she was after promotion, just from the look of her walls!'

The visual dimension of the classroom is, however, worth considering in the light of alternative points of view since it is through the sense of sight that the majority of children learn most. The senses provide the raw data which is rationalised and interpreted at a cognitive level or which is classified and categorised in relation to existing knowledge. Of the five senses it is the information received visually which is most easily interpreted by most sighted people. It is the most lasting and is most easily related to other sensory experiences. The predominance of sight is also conveyed in everyday phrases such as, 'I saw it with my own eyes,' when talking to a sceptical companion, or, 'I'll believe that when I see it.'

What the children learn from the displays put up in their school is not restricted to the information presented by the displayed material. The messages conveyed to the children by the teacher's choice of items to display are many and complex, but fundamentally the teacher is indicating her/his approval of the work and offering a model of what she/he sees as good practice to the class and the wider school community. Publicising the desired model amounts to taking control of what children will value. 'Publicity is the culture of the consumer society. It propagates through images that society's belief in itself' (Berger, 1972, p.139). Children entering the community of the school quickly discover what is valued in the society they have joined.

The following case studies illustrate the effect of the visual dimension of the school environment on the learning behaviour and attitudes of two groups of children. The student teacher and English teacher who were working with the children began to revise their own views of the purpose and power of display, and discovered ways of making the medium work for them to enhance the educational experience they were able to offer their classes.

The first study focusses on a Year 5 and 6 junior class and a student on her final teaching practice. The subject of the second study is a secondary school English teacher, who introduces display in the classes of boys she works with from Year 7 to Year 12 in a comprehensive school.

Case Study 1: Ellen's final teaching practice

I supervised Ellen when she undertook the second and final teaching practice of the PGCE year. Her first practice with Year 3 children had been a success, and she was looking forward to working with a group of older juniors, in a vertically grouped Year 5 and 6 class. The location of the school was a pleasant home counties suburb – quite a change from the council estate catchment of her first school experience. Ellen was placed with a class teacher who also had responsibility for art and display in the school, and additionally who was to be acting deputy head during the term when the teaching practice took place. Ellen's degree background was in engineering, and she had undertaken her 'curriculum specialism' work in the area of primary design and technology. She saw as an advantage this opportunity to work with a teacher who could offer a creative/artistic dimension to design work.

In a pre-practice tutorial, Ellen described her first impressions of the school she was to work in.

> The displays are absolutely stunning. The whole school's like it. I hope my work will be good enough to match up to their standards.

In the same tutorial Ellen voiced her concern at her class teacher's characterisation of the class as 'difficult', and her advice to 'sit on them firmly'. I reassured her that most problems of control and discipline can be remedied by ensuring that the children are motivated and interested, with work which is well organised and challenging. The preliminary preparation Ellen had already undertaken suggested that ideas and lesson planning would not be a cause for concern.

On my first visit to Ellen three days into the practice I too was impressed with the beautiful displays of art work in the school, not only in the classroom, but in the entrance, hall and corridors. I commented upon them to the headteacher, who agreed that Mrs M, Ellen's class teacher, certainly had a gift for display, and that it was due to her help that every teacher now aspired to the highest standards of presentation.

In the classroom, Ellen struggled to settle her class for a creative writing session. The control problem was finally solved by the arrival of Mrs M, who installed herself in a corner with the computer for a while, whilst Ellen introduced her lesson and got the children started. After the departure of the class teacher the children became increasingly restless, and Ellen tried various strategies to calm them, with limited effect. The following is an extract from my notes to her.

> The idea and your introduction were basically good. Sensible strategy to keep moving round the tables offering encouragement. Reading Darren's work aloud did seem to encourage the others and to calm them. Think therefore about the effect of giving the children a real purpose and audience for their work – a class book, perhaps, or a display of the finished stories. Putting your book away in your desk after you have finished does not exactly inspire anyone to greater efforts!

Ellen reflected thoughtfully on the lesson in her written evaluation, and concluded:

> In future I must try to ensure the children know what will happen

to the writing afterwards, and that they understand that it will be read by someone other than me.

The following week I visited Ellen again, and observed a Maths lesson, in which several interesting practical investigations had been set up for the children. The class was, on the whole, less than co-operative. It seemed to me that they had sufficient work of sufficient interest, and that the lesson was well structured and organised. I noted from reading the teaching practice file that many teaching sessions had been less than successful, in Ellen's opinion, due to problems of control.

Notable exceptions were an art session and some design technology work in which the children had been making a model village. A discussion with the class teacher at the end of the visit concluded with her advising Ellen that she simply must be much more firm with the children and 'get them under your thumb'. I agreed to return at the end of the week to see an art/craft session.

The next visit was a revelation. The children settled to the art activities quietly and willingly, and Ellen and I circulated amongst them offering help as needed. The atmosphere in the room was totally calm and tranquil. One child, who had been particularly awkward during my previous visit, chatted pleasantly with me and told me he hoped his work would be put up in the entrance hall. I noticed some practical maths work, which had been under way on my previous visit, mounted and placed on a side bench apparently ready to go up on the wall. I noted in the teaching practice file that Ellen had planned to display the work. My note to Ellen praised the lesson, commented upon the children's behaviour and remarked that the maths work would make an effective display.

In our discussion later Ellen expressed her disappointment that the class teacher had asked her not to display the maths work, but rather to mount some pictures, which would 'look nicer'. She added that she had noticed the only work which was ever displayed was decorative and that this was the case throughout the school. We speculated upon the extent to which this might affect the children's attitude to their work in other curriculum areas. When Mrs M joined us I remarked on the fact that the maths work was ready to go up, and that I would look forward to seeing it displayed on my next visit.

The following week, I took the opportunity to chat to other teachers in the staff room. I complimented them on the beautiful work on the walls. It was interesting to note that all the teachers responsible for the display work viewed their efforts as the result of a 'common sense' approach, combined with 'inspiration' from Mrs M. They did not regard themselves as having been instructed or persuaded to work as they did, neither did they see their work as different from display work in any other 'good' school. From my observation I had to agree that the only work displayed was indeed art, craft or decorative items. In Ellen's classroom I was pleased to see the maths work pinned up, and a class book of stories in preparation. Ellen introduced her science session by telling the children that their graphical presentations of results would go on the wall only if they were neat enough. The children undertook the practical activities with the minimum of fuss and worked fairly diligently on their recording. The teaching practice file reported a small improvement in children's conduct in both maths and language sessions.

As the teaching practice progressed, Ellen persevered with her efforts to display work from a range of curriculum areas, and the children gradually became more co-operative. Indeed, by the last week of the practice, the question of control was no longer an issue, and my notes to her instead focussed upon details of the display.

> Whilst the wall by the window looks wonderful from a distance, with items beautifully balanced and spaced, I really think that something which is supposed to be read should be pinned up straight rather than at an odd angle. Also think about the eye-level of the reader – save pictures for high and low, and keep writing in the centre. The green leaf shaped mounts are most effective for the 'tree' poems. The shades of green you have used give unity to the display.

At the end of the practice the class teacher declared herself well satisfied with Ellen's progress and commented favourably upon the appearance of the room. She reserved her most fulsome praise for the art, craft and design work, and commended Ellen for finally managing to 'squash those little horrors'.

The extent to which the change in the philosophy of display in this particular classroom actually influenced the children's attitude, level of motivation and conduct may be debated. Without doubt the quality of the work and intrinsic interest it held for them played a part. Window-dressing alone is unlikely to bring about the change in behaviour which was apparent here. However, Ellen and I both remain convinced that giving status to work from all areas of the curriculum by displaying it as well and as sensitively as possible did, in this class, help to motivate the children, which in turn led to fewer problems of class control and discipline.

Case Study 2: display in a new context

I was asked to run a one-day INSET course on spelling and hand-writing for the special needs and English departments of a boys' comprehensive secondary school last year. The invitation was issued by Jackie E, an ex-colleague of mine from several years previously who had recently moved to a teaching post in the English department of that school. One of the first things which struck her on starting in her new position was the drabness of the environment and the apparent lack of care anyone – staff or pupils – had for the appearance of their workplace.

> The staffroom's tatty, the classrooms are grim, the whole school is just so uncared for, it's quite depressing just walking round. My other school was so fresh and pleasant by comparison. It's probably just because it's all boys, I suppose. No-one seems to bother about what the place looks like.

During her first term, Jackie made several other observations about her new school. One concerned the policy (or rather the custom and practice, there being no policy) about display in the school. The only departments which ever displayed any of the pupils' work were the art department and the craft, design and technology department, the latter restricting its efforts to open days and parents' evenings. The large areas of grey pinboarding in all the rooms remained bare, except for lists of school teams and with the times for sports practices making occasional appearances. Another of her observations was the lack of concern the boys showed for the general tidiness and appearance of their classrooms, constantly leaving her base room in disarray, frequently leaving it strewn with their own belongings which they later complained about losing. They also seemed to take little pride in the presentation and appearance of their work, which, Jackie noted, reflected the appearance of their working environment. Discussions with colleagues led Jackie to discover that several members of staff were concerned about the general standard of presentation of the pupils' work, particularly the poor quality of handwriting and spelling. This was felt to be the joint responsibility of the school's English and special needs sections, and it seemed appropriate to the two departments that their next INSET day should focus upon the topic of 'presentation'.

My programme for the day included practical advice on helping the boys to develop strategies for improving spelling, and activities to support the development of handwriting skills. A common thread which ran through the day was an emphasis upon teachers providing an authentic audience and a real purpose for the pupils' written work, as both would act as strong motivators to improve the appearance of finished pieces. Included in the programme was a slide presentation of examples of completed work, mainly from primary school children, much of it photographed as it was displayed on classroom walls. Several of the staff agreed with Jackie that displaying some of their pupils' work would possibly prove worthwhile and help them in achieving their goal of improving their pupils' attitude to presentation, handwriting and spelling. Jackie confided later that in her opinion part of the problem was rooted in the lack of concern evident in the school for the appearance of the classrooms.

> If it's obvious no-one is worried about the look of their working environment why should the boys bother about the presentation of their work? The English department at least is going to have to smarten up.

Over the course of the next two terms Jackie worked to develop and foster in the pupils she was working with a concern for the presentation of their work. She started with the Year 7 classes, hoping to 'stop the rot' before it had really started. A major feature of the campaign was to offer them a sense of audience for their written work by displaying as much of it as possible in the English base rooms. The displays of written work were supplemented by pieces of art work and posters made by the boys in their own time. Her 'A' level group commented upon the displayed work, and asked whether they could have a display board for their group's work. Jackie readily agreed, and by the end of the first term the appearance of all the English rooms had been transformed, two of Jackie's colleagues having also joined in the project. The second term saw the extension of the policy to all year groups, and the work itself began to move out of the English section into other areas of the school building. I returned to the school on a social occasion several months later, and noted and commented upon the change in the appearance of the rooms.

Jackie and her colleagues discussed the effect of their efforts on the pupils' work and attitudes.

S.   A lot of them have really made an effort with the work they have put up. Their books are not really that much better though, in some cases.

J.   We've probably got to accept that not every piece of work will be done to presentation standard. It's not really necessary, after all. As long as we and they know they can do it when they need to, we're getting somewhere. They are taking much more pride in presentation generally, and actually about things like spelling too.

P.   I think I have detected a bit more concern about the state of the rooms. Year 7 are definitely less slob-like these days!

The staff were, on the whole, pleased with the outcome of the two terms' work. The pupils' work and their attitude to its presentation had in many cases noticeably improved, and there were some indications, although tentative, that attitudes to the general appearance of the English rooms were more positive.

It seemed worthwhile to discover from the boys themselves how they felt about the development in their working practice in English. The staff were happy for me to discuss this with their classes. Informal interviews were held with individuals from Year 7 and Year 12 (sixth form). Some of their comments reflected the perceptions of their teachers, but one or two points made by the pupils had not been noted by the staff. The boys were asked: 'Does it make any difference to your work if you know it's going on the wall?'

A Year 7 boy:

I actually enjoy doing the work much more if I know I can do some art work to go with it. If your stuff's going on the wall you can generally do a poster to go with it. Miss lets us put things up we do at home if it's to do with the English.

His classmate:

I definitely try harder to get it looking neat and that when it's for the display. It takes you longer, but you feel good if you know yours is one of the best. I never liked English much in the juniors, but my writing's much better now and I'm better at getting it looking tidy. I like doing maps and things to go with it, that makes it more interesting. You can show people what you mean sometimes with a map or a diagram or something about the writing or the book. We don't generally do that in our books, just for the wall.

A Year 12 pupil:

Stuff we've done for the boards has generally been on a much larger scale than you would normally work to, and we've done it in a pair or a group usually. It's good to do something that plots something out visually and do it with someone else so you can get their ideas as well. Helps you work things out a bit sometimes.

A Year 12 pupil from another group:

We want to make our board the best. We try as a group to get all our work looking brilliant, which of course it is! But yes, I think you do work harder, partly so you don't let the group down, or let yourself down. Your name's up on show as well.

The twin purposes of introducing display were to try to provide a sense of audience for the pupils' work to motivate them to take care with presentation and to improve the general appearance of the rooms they were working in. Jackie and her colleagues were happy that they had made a successful beginning to their campaign. Without realising it, this English department had also helped to develop links between some of the pupils' home and outside interests and their curriculum work in English. They had helped individuals who perhaps struggled to express in words exactly what they meant, to find other ways of expressing their ideas. They had encouraged collaboration and the development of thinking around a common topic whilst working on joint projects, and had begun, with at least one of their groups, to foster a sense of community and a feeling of pride in a job well done. Jackie considered these findings, and agreed that indeed, the display campaign had achieved more than expected.

All the extra things are actually the sort of things we try to achieve through activities like Drama and debates. I just hadn't realised what a powerful medium wall displays can be for the exchange and development of ideas.

Discussion

The importance of visual perception in education has already been highlighted. A plea by Rousseau as long ago as the eighteenth century for a form of education not centred solely on words, but taking into account children's reactions to their surroundings supports this view. It has been shown that display, far from being merely decorative, can have a significant part to play in the learning process. Teachers, therefore, should know why display is important and how to get the most out of it.

In both the case study schools, the wall displays appeared to act as relayers of attitudes, beliefs and principles intentionally or unintentionally underlying aspects of the curriculum on offer. This may not be particularly surprising, but what is, is finding that whilst children are acutely sensitive to messages embedded in displays, many of their teachers are not aware either of what is being relayed or of their part in the transmission process. From Case Study 2 it seems that even those teachers who are aware of the ways in which display can influence children's attitudes may be surprised at some of the effects of displaying work. These were revealed by the college tutor, who, wishing to pursue the topic further, interviewed some of the boys who had been involved in the project. Without this intervention, these insights would have been lost.

The case studies do not consider the whole range of visual aids to education, therefore the importance and use of such things as television, video, film, overhead projector and blackboard will not be addressed here. Neither will the role of display in the field of tactile experience be addressed in depth. The term 'display' is taken to mean anything which is exhibited in the classroom. In determining what is and what is not display, it is the intention behind the items displayed that is important, and not only the items themselves. For instance, covering a cracked or discoloured board or section of the wall with colourful paper would not be display, but that same paper pinned on the wall as an illustration of colour or texture would. The difference is in the intention. 'Why was it put up?' is the crucial question. This was asked by the college supervisor in Case Study 1 as she worked with Ellen, who was gradually developing her own understanding of the power of display. One of the most important things about material on display is that it should be put up for a real purpose, and not simply to decorate a wall or cover an old table.

If the validity of this claim is accepted, the assertion that all display material must have a recognised purpose becomes a very interesting and powerful one, having far-reaching implications as to how teachers should select and assess what they display.

If it is accepted that display material should serve a purpose, display becomes a means to an end, rather than an end in itself. Therefore all items for display, children's work as well as teachers' contributions, should be judged according to their effectiveness in meeting their purpose and not on their own intrinsic qualities.

This is fundamentally a utilitarian or functionalist view.

It may be helpful at this point to classify the kind of displays most usually seen in schools into three main areas:

1. teacher produced

2. displays which are initiated by the teacher but evolve as dialogues between the class and teacher

3. displays of children's work, mounted and arranged by the teacher or by the children themselves.

All are important, but all require to be justified in some way other than through their ability to fill a space, or cover the walls for open day or the visit of the college examiner. For instance all display material, whatever its purpose, should help to create a stimulating, attractive and exciting environment in which the children will be encouraged to work to their full potential. All teachers and students involved in both the case studies would agree with that. However, different types of display can serve different purposes. Some will be intended to arouse interest in a particular theme or topic, others to communicate factual information of one kind or another, and yet others to reward children for effort and hard work. The precise nature of the purpose of each display will vary, but whatever the type of display, it is as a medium for the exchange of information and ideas, both overt and hidden, that display is most important. Students and teachers must be helped to recognise and identify a purpose for their displays, and initially may need the guidance and support of a tutor in making the kind of choices which have to be made for displays to meet effectively the needs of their classes.

It has already been noted that some teachers use display to communicate to a class a general standard of excellence to which the class should aspire. More specifically, and much more usefully, a teacher, through careful selection of the best pieces of work from each child may provide an individual and attainable standard at which to aim. The selection of work for display requires sensitivity and thought, as well as a detailed knowledge of the potential of the children responsible for it. Items, therefore, should be chosen in relation to the pupils' personal abilities rather than to a standard some members of the class are unable to meet.

This fits in with a point made earlier that whether or not something is suitable for display depends not upon its quality *per se*, but upon its usefulness. If one always chose the 'best' pieces of children's work to display, those children who inevitably never have any of their work on the wall may become disillusioned. It would not be surprising if such children lost interest in school and schoolwork. The possibility of children being 'turned off' entire curriculum areas from which no work was ever put up was suggested in Case Study 1. However, Ellen was supported and guided by her tutor when selecting children's work to display, and asked herself not, 'How attractive is it?', but, 'What can I achieve through displaying this piece of work rather than that?' Her class were subsequently encouraged and motivated to work to their own particular potential in a range of curriculum areas. Conversely, a teacher who uncritically selected the 'best' pieces of work without reference to what each child was capable of, could choose to display the work of an able child which was below his or her best, and thus encourage a complacent attitude.

Teachers should also be aware that as children move from one schematic stage to another, their work – in the sense of the end result – may deteriorate as their ideas outstrip their skills. A Year 7 boy in Case Study 2 comments that he did not care much for English in the junior school, but things are better now his handwriting has improved. One could dare to speculate that he received little praise for his untidy, poorly scribed efforts at that time also. However, such work may still be worth displaying in order to encourage the children to continue breaking new ground. Similarly, teachers should try to encourage those children who experiment and whose work is perhaps less neat because of it than that of children who stick to tried and tested methods. It is the display's purpose to exhibit the interesting and innovative work of the children, not to provide pretty pictures for the display. The work is of primary importance, and children should not be asked to produce work merely to stick on the wall. In both case studies the confidence to make such choices was developed with the support of the college tutor. She was able to see beyond the 'here and now' in each school situation and identified a fundamental need to encourage revisions in the thinking of both the student and the teachers involved.

It is also important that children be given frequent opportunities to select, mount and display their own work, and that they come to regard this aspect as part of the work itself. Classrooms in which children are involved in controlling what is displayed almost always have about them a freshness which is absent from totally teacher-controlled environments. As window dressers and the advertising industry well know, the human eye is only too ready to accept visual stimuli as part of the landscape. The same can sometimes be true of classrooms. There are classrooms where the teacher changes the displays regularly, but which never really look any different. Some of the classrooms in the Case Study 1 school came into this category. In order to maintain visual impact, not only the items and kinds of items displayed but the design and dimension of the displays should change frequently. Displays put up by or influenced by children inevitably give rise to a greater variety of styles of presentation and frequently generate more interest than those which are teacher produced.

Displays put up by the teacher should where possible allow for additional contributions from the children so that they can develop and expand in those areas that the children are most interested in. Case Study 2 describes the enthusiasm of some Year 7 children to add pictures and posters to their writing display. By developing their own displays they gain benefit from the numerous opportunities to consider their own work and that of others in a critical light.

This leads naturally into a debate on the aesthetic dimension of display. Displays put up for aesthetic reasons can be justified within a functionalist framework, provided that aesthetic considerations do not predominate nor are allowed to subvert other important functions of display. Aesthetic qualities are not unimportant. Indeed, any display's aesthetic qualities are not only vital in enabling the display to meet its purpose of informing and stimulating the children, but can also be justified for their own sake, as long as their worth is not internalised, but expressed in terms of their effect on those who perceive them. It is what happens within the minds and imaginations of those who look at and touch the display that is important and not the display itself. For instance, a teacher would not be justified in putting up a print of a Cezanne painting in the classroom merely because she liked it, but would be justified if she thought the picture would encourage an appreciation of and interest in art in the children. It would not matter if the picture had no effect on the children, so long as the teacher had recognised the essential function of display, that is, as a medium and not an end result. Aesthetic considerations can therefore play a dual role in display. They may be positive if used to attract the children's attention or to provide them with opportunities to consider critically and appreciate the relationships between materials, colour, shape and texture. Or they may be negative if allowed to become predominant and all important. Ellen, in Case Study 1, became aware of the negative role of aesthetic considerations early in her practice. Her supervisor was able to guide her in her campaign to adopt an alternative philosophy for displaying material in her room.

So far, most of this discussion has been 'classroom based', in that a display's worth has been assessed according to its impact on the children. However, one should not forget that display also has a role to play in informing the wider school community of fellow teachers, parents and governors of what is going on. It is here that the major area of conflict between the positive and negative applications of aesthetic values can arise.

Most teachers, and certainly all primary school teachers, must at one time or another, have felt the pressure to 'get something on the wall'. That pressure may have been applied by those in authority, who, having recognised the positive purposes to which display can be put, are encouraging others to show that they are aware of it too. Alternatively, the pressure may come from those who are less well informed, and judge what goes on in classrooms by the quality of the 'window-dressing'. Either way, whether it is an impending OFSTED visit or a looming parents' evening, the effect is the same. Displays are rushed up to satisfy the audience rather than to stimulate, encourage and inform the pupils.

It is interesting to note that the amount and quality of display material produced is linked with the intrinsic worth of the individual as a teacher. The display has become personalised – but it is no longer that of the class, a collective and collaborative effort, but that of the teacher. The quality and quantity of the displays are taken as a sort of currency or measure of relative status within the school.

The judges whom teachers fear will find them wanting are not the children, but on the one hand their colleagues, headteachers, school governors and children's parents and, on the other, inspectors and advisers. This shift in emphasis is important, as it causes the display's purpose to change, and consequently its nature changes also. The desire to make an aesthetically pleasing spectacle becomes predominant. Mrs M the class teacher in Case Study 1 asked Ellen not to display her maths work, as some pictures would 'look nicer'. In this case, 'What will look good?' had become the determining factor, and, since there was no other purpose in mind, the more important questions – 'What are you trying to achieve?' and 'How can you best do it?' would never have arisen without the intervention of the college supervisor. Such a philosophy in fact bypasses the issue of the value of process in children's work and offers the children a biased view of the significance and role of some aspects of the curriculum. The only thing that matters is the appearance of the end product.

Thus aesthetic considerations can have a negative impact. Indeed, they may even lead to the situation of the teacher 'doing it for' the children, or 'doctoring' their work before putting it on display. It would hardly be surprising if the messages children received from such practices led them to doubt the value of their own efforts.

It has been argued that any display, whether teacher-produced or child-produced, must have a justification which goes beyond the material's superficial qualities and look at its effects or intended effects. Adopting the position that schools themselves are sites where 'cultural reproduction' readily occurs (Bernstein 1977), the hidden messages conveyed by the visual environment must also be remembered. Displays may act as springboards to further activities, or help to create positive attitudes towards school and schoolwork within individual children. An appreciation of the role, importance and power of display is therefore a valuable asset to any teacher.

Conclusions

The community of the school can say things to children in a great variety of ways, display being just one of them. The case studies illustrate the ways in which subtle messages carried by displays can be decoded by the children in ways not only relevant to the immediate 'here and now' but in wider and more general contexts.

Teachers, as members of the school community, are not always aware of the influence of the displays they put up or of the kinds of messages they are transmitting. A college tutor was able to lead the teachers in the secondary school in Case Study 2 to a greater appreciation of the power of display as a medium for teaching and learning. Those teachers already understood a good deal about the function of display as a motivating force, unlike some of the staff at the primary school in Case Study 1, who saw displays as classroom decoration. The role of the HE tutor was crucial there in helping the student to break through the 'attitude barrier' presented by the class teacher. That the supervising tutor came from outside the school community is an important feature in this case. Not only was she able to see beyond the window dressing, but she was more able to challenge the class teacher than someone from within the school. A teacher-mentor, even one who had identified and accepted the problem encountered by the student, may not have had the confidence or authority to override the opinion of a teacher who was her superior and who was a very dominant force in the school. 'Swimming against the tide' in a school tends to be discouraged. Teacher colleagues have to work together once student teaching

112

practice is over, and implied criticism of colleagues tends not to be well received.

Once teachers and students understand and appreciate the influence of displays they can exploit the educational uses and the social functions of the medium. Without this understanding, displays put up in classrooms can have as many negative effects as positive ones.

References

Berger, J. (1972) *Ways of seeing*. London: BBC Publications/Penguin.
Bernstein, B. (1977) *Class, codes and control. Vol. 3: Towards a theory of educational transmissions* (2nd revised edn). London: Routledge and Kegan Paul.
Daniels, H. (1989) 'Visual displays as tacit relays of the structure of pedagogic practice', *British Journal of Sociology of Education*, **10** (2), pp.123–40.

CHAPTER 7

Enquiring into the Arts: Teaching Drama to Students and to Pupils

Tom Sweeney and Robert Catt

Introduction

Two PGCE primary students sit awaiting the arrival of a course colleague who will shortly join them by occupying the empty chair which has been set slightly apart in preparation for the visitor. They are not relaxed; they appear on edge, formal, even severe. One student holds a clip board with writing pad; the other will soon begin to pace around the chairs. The third student has now arrived; she is also on edge. She sits and looks expectantly, anxiously, to her colleagues. She is nervous because an interrogation is about to begin.

These three students are in role: two are detectives and the third is a suspect in a fictional investigation. The suspect is about to be questioned but she is not unprepared. She has spent some ten minutes with two colleagues, also in role as suspects, generating, planning and rehearsing a collaboratively prepared alibi based on an imagined crime. It is intense work, they have a tight deadline, so they need to support each other in this preparation.

There is also tension in the fictional interview room during this preparatory period; the students in role as detectives are also under pressure. They are expected to produce results; a demanding superior (the tutor in role) is an additional source of stress. These students also take the work seriously; they carefully consider the style and content of their questioning. They must organise the space appropriately; to accommodate the suspect, or perhaps to intimidate the suspect. They must plan their approach: it might be one of sympathetic nods, or it might be aggressive pacing, or a deliberately perplexing blend of each. They must decide who will record the interview and how this should be done.

The interrogation begins; there are few smiles!

This is a 'snapshot' of a drama project undertaken with a group of PGCE students. They are midway through their one-year course of professional training. The first block teaching practice has been successfully completed by these students, but a second practice which is both longer and more rigorously assessed still awaits them. The drama project is part of a wider unit of work on drama as part of a wider programme of 'English in Education'. The 'detectives' project focusses on enquiry skills and the strategies that teachers can develop to enable Key Stage 2 pupils to become confident and effective users of spoken language.

In this chapter we aim to explore some dilemmas that arise concerning the professional preparation of teachers of drama, English and the arts. We intend to focus on a particular case of drama teaching in order to ground our observations, insights and conclusions in the reality of practice in HE. Events are described; planning is exposed and made explicit; analysis for relevant meaning is attempted. Our intention is to open a window on HE practice, allowing those colleagues working in schools with an interest in ITE to view a particular case. This is not presented as exemplar material but in a spirit of enquiry and developing partnership. It is also seen as contributing to established frameworks of action research in HE. Zuber-Skerritt's attempt to integrate theory and practice in HE through educational research and teaching, provides a helpful starting point for this enquiry.

> My intention is not to develop a 'grand theory' in higher education, but to describe, explain and improve learning, teaching and staff development in a particular context. Each reader will have to decide which of the phenomena described and which of the principles developed ... would apply to his/her own situation.
> (Zuber-Skerritt 1992, p.128)

Moreover, the term 'window on practice' is a useful reminder that those on the inside of HE must also be prepared to look outside and, in this case, acknowledge and value the work of schools and the importance of a dynamic and mutually supporting relationship between theory and practice in schools and in colleges.

(i)

Approaches to research

The enquiry processes on which this chapter is based have involved tutors who are still relatively inexperienced in the formal traditions of educational research. Although carefully planned, systematically organised and technically competent, the processes and outcomes have nevertheless proved open-ended and have revealed more than we anticipated.

Paradigms of research

Our methodological approach resides in that tradition of educational research which has been termed naturalistic, descriptive, interpretative and non-positivistic. We are not concerned with large-scale surveys, statistical analyses, measurements nor the collection of data with the intention of producing clear, discernible patterns. We did not begin by generating a hypothesis nor do we intend to conclude with solutions. Rather, our intention has been to 'get inside' a piece of teaching and learning in HE, to shed light on the processes involved, to illuminate our practice.

In setting out to examine a particular aspect of our teaching we found it necessary to consider three dimensions. First, the nature of the work in which we were involved, in this case arts education and drama in the curriculum. Subjectivity in the arts is an accepted part of those essential processes of engagement with this area of learning. Qualitative accounts, unlike quantitative ones, involve interpretation, acknowledging the possibility of alternative viewpoints, and provide a logical approach to portraying this way of working.

A second dimension concerns the importance of our own professional training and recent experience in schools. To ensure the project was rooted in recent practice a pilot project was undertaken in a local primary school. A number of drama sessions were taught by a tutor and these were expertly recorded through video and still photography. This ensured two advantages: namely, evidence of the practicality of the proposed tasks and activities for

Key Stage 2 pupils; and evidence of the tutors' direct experience of teaching the proposed material. This was intended to establish principles of practical insight into the proposed content and to explore and recommend teaching strategies to students on a PGCE primary course.

Third, the intended audience for this enquiry and the potential for action research of this kind in professional development was a further consideration. In targeting an audience of practitioners it is necessary to address issues of readability and accessibility. Much has been written about the 'closed shop' of educational research and the alienating effect this has on teachers. Our intention is to describe events and discuss issues that have meaning for practitioners and to do this in a way that has communicative power.

Case studies

With these three dimensions in mind — that is, artistic content, school-located activity and an audience of practitioners — it seemed appropriate to adopt a case study approach to the investigation. Within the case study, a broadly 'illuminative' stance is taken, which owes much to the traditions of investigative journalism and documentary film making. Groundwater-Smith has directly addressed the issue of accessibility in her discussion of the portrayal of educational experiences through the use of literary non-fiction, 'new journalism' and the 'metaphor of the story as photograph'.

> The portrayer of educational events may become at one and the same time the 'camera', the 'photographer' and the story-teller. The notion of the photograph is the medium for fixing on the object or event to be described, while the story is the agent for transforming and interpreting that event for others.
> (Groundwater-Smith 1984, p.5)

The use of a camera in our investigation is taken in both its metaphorical sense and also literal sense through the extensive employment of video equipment and still photography. As a means of recording both sound and vision this has been our major tool in collecting relevant data. Not only does this facilitate systematic analysis of actions, words and body language (especially important in the area of drama in education), but also produces archive material that is readily available for further research by ourselves and other interested parties. Whilst acknowledging the camera's potential to influence the course of events, the advantage of access to a trained operator and appropriate equipment both during filming and for post-production analysis outweighed the possibility of serious distortion.

Consequently, a series of teaching events were planned and were undertaken in four distinct stages:

● *Stage 1:* a pilot project consisting of a session led by a tutor in an outer London primary school with a mixed group of Year 5 and 6 pupils

● *Stage 2:* a series of drama activities with PGCE primary students as part of their college-based 'English in Education' programme

● *Stage 3:* a separate discussion session with the same group of PGCE students with a tutor leading a discussion on the evaluation of the drama workshop

● *Stage 4:* a student-led drama lesson with Year 6 pupils in an outer London primary school during a final TP.

Each of these sessions was filmed by an experienced video technician who was accompanied by one of the tutors as an extra camera operator during the college-based workshop in order to capture simultaneous group activity. The pilot project was also recorded with still photography.

(ii)

The drama project and its teaching

Drama is not a foundation subject in the National Curriculum, but it is, nevertheless, continuing to make an impact both as a subject in its own right and as a method of learning. A wall poster (NCC 1992) rather than a ring binder may not be such a bad thing if it enables teachers to introduce drama activities to their classes without some of the attendant pressures of statutory orders. For the resourceful, even if inexperienced teacher, there are ample, helpful and substantial contributions from a number of sources (for example, Arts Council 1992; DES 1989; Hornbrook 1991; NCC 1990; Neelands 1992; Woolland 1993) which indicate how drama can be used in the developing context of the school curriculum.

The non-statutory guidance for English in the National Curriculum also gives some useful advice on the strategies that can be effective in using drama in the classroom, hall or studio. The increasing use of role-play, for example, is evidence of the growing interest in active learning approaches. The welcome emphasis upon speaking and listening in recent years has enabled teachers to give more attention to situation, audience and the variety of discourse when providing children with purposeful contexts for learning and when making assessments.

Our work with both pupils in schools and students of education frequently involves role-play and simulation, which can yield impressive results. Primary colleagues with knowledge of drama in the classroom will be familiar with many of the approaches associated with drama in education. Our intention was to enable PGCE students with little drama experience to be confident in adopting some of these drama techniques.

'Detectives', the name given to the drama project, was a unit of work which we used successfully with both children and adults. It needs subtle adjustments to meet individual and situational circumstances but it has the potential for flexible and creative development. The programme is designed to span about three one-hour drama sessions and, if possible, should occupy a spacious area – a drama studio or hall rather than a classroom. However, like many drama ideas, in the hands of an imaginative teacher there are a number of variations possible which would work within a classroom and within different time allocations.

The description that follows is an overview of the project and can be read as the basic planning framework which was followed in all the taught sessions during Stages 1, 2 and 4. Therefore the plan was used by the tutor and student teacher with PGCE students and primary pupils alike. Not unsurprisingly, there were differences, variations and developments, and where significant, these will be discussed when dealing with each separate stage of the case study.

Establishing a context

Participants enter the hall/studio and are asked to sit in a prepared circle. The teacher, in role, introduces himself as a police training officer and establishes the context of a detectives' training school by welcoming the would-be sleuths to a training course. In turn, he invites introductions from each participant, providing examples and prompts where necessary.

The ability to recall names, places, times, numbers and so on, is stressed as an important skill for detectives to acquire; the first of a series of tests and challenges begins with a name game and is followed by some observation tasks. At this stage every effort is made to ensure all police officers pass the first tests giving the training officer the opportunity to praise the high calibre of recruit on this particular course.

Telling stories

This phase of the work is introduced, briefly, by reminding the participants, in role as police officers, that the accurate recall of information is a vital skill for all good detectives. There are times when this can be aided through the use of notes but on other occasions, such as 'undercover' work, this is not possible.

In pairs, as police officers, one partner tells a brief story based on a past 'case'. The teacher explains that, shortly, A will be telling B a brief story. Emphasis is now placed upon clarity and cohesion of narrative and the importance of active listening is also stressed. (We found it useful to discuss with participants the ways in which detectives make notes; some participants find it useful to mime note-making or to pretend they are using a small cassette recorder.) Once the story is told it is then reported as accurately as possible by the listener to a new partner. This may be undertaken by participants two or three times.

The teacher intervenes by inviting one of the police officers to volunteer to tell the version of the story she/he has just heard. (It may be possible to set this up as if it were a junior officer reporting to a superior.) Once again, accurate recall is emphasised. Does anyone recognise that version as 'her/his' original story? What has happened to it during its journey around the room? Why have these changes occurred? This can be repeated with as many offerings as circumstances allow. The teacher then sums up this phase of the course by drawing the attention of police officers to the importance of accurate and detailed recall of information.

Planning and exploring alibis

The alibi activity is the next element of the programme and is the main focus of the 'detectives' project. As an introduction to this phase the 'police officers' are reminded that as detectives they will spend much of their time asking clear and searching questions as part of the processes of investigation and inquiry. In order to improve these inquiry skills 'police officers' will now be asked to take part in a simulation exercise which will develop their interview techniques. As is often the case with police training some participants will be asked to take the role of suspects.

Participants are grouped in fives (but variations in group size can work equally well). Each group is briskly subdivided as three suspects and two detectives. Suspects will be asked to work together to construct an agreed story – an alibi – in which they must account in detail for their movements between 6.00 p.m. and 9.00 p.m. on the previous Saturday evening, for example. Meanwhile, detectives will be expected to prepare questions which will test the veracity of the suspects' alibis.

The teacher explains the interview procedure: suspects will be interviewed individually by both detectives and will have no subsequent opportunities for further collaboration; a strict time limit will be enforced for the length of each interview.

In their separate groups, suspects invent and prepare a detailed account of their whereabouts between 6.00 p.m. and 9.00 p.m. last Saturday evening; simultaneously, detectives prepare their questions. The teacher should allow about ten minutes for this preparatory discussion.

During this time the teacher can also take the opportunity to carry out some further briefing of the detectives. The relative value of different approaches to the interview can be discussed with the detectives, including turn-taking, specific roles and responsibilities and such important details as the organisation of the working space and furniture for the interview. Similarly, the teacher will need to direct sample questions at the suspects to give them a flavour of what they might expect from the detectives. Suspects should be reminded to give meticulous attention to points of detail.

Interviewing suspects

As the preparation period is brought to an end the teacher reminds groups that exactly two minutes are allowed for each interview. Questioning the first suspects is then undertaken by detectives until the teacher brings the interviews to an end and asks interviewed suspects to move to the far end of the studio/classroom/hall where they sit facing away from the central activity. Once this is done the next interview begins; two-minute interviews are repeated for all the suspects.

Discovering discrepancies

Separately and then collectively the detectives and the suspects should review the accounts given in order to check their corroboration.

The teacher invites the suspects to join their relevant detectives reforming the original group of five. Paired detectives are asked to give their decisions – suspects to be released or detained – together with an account of the interviews and reasons for their decision. They are also asked to comment on the suspects' abilities to answer questions.

The teacher, in turn, invites suspects to comment on the style and effectiveness of the detectives' questions.

'Passing-out ceremony'

The teacher invites participants to re-make the original circle. To enhance the confidence-building nature of the programme, the session ends with the teacher, still in role as the training officer, complimenting the participants on their work and informing them of their success in completing the course. It might, of course, be appropriate to enact a passing-out ceremony, to include the awarding of certificates or meeting the 'chief training officer' or a combination of these and other ideas.

The teacher, now out of role, has the opportunity to reflect upon the sessions and, in turn, invite comments from the participants. It is our experience that, in addition to its value as a discrete unit of work, the 'detectives project' has considerable developmental potential. Obvious opportunities for writing are also presented – preparing and phrasing questions, descriptions and reports, for example – but the programme should be of greatest value in supporting speaking and listening.

(iii)

Stages of research

In this section there follows a more analytical description of each stage of the case study. The intention is to indicate how the project developed as a piece of professional training which was rooted in primary practice and was intended to prepare students for final teaching practice and more long-term demands when working in primary schools as newly qualified teachers. Essential similarities can be traced through each teaching event but there are also important differences to be noted, especially in the presentation of material to the students. The intention is to establish firmly the principle of experiential learning so that students are in a position to gain insights into pupil achievement in drama and their own personal and professional development.

In order to structure the accumulated data into a coherent account we have used a framework for analysis which focusses on four aspects of the 'detectives project' and corresponds to the general teaching plan of each session at Stages 1, 2 and 3. These four aspects are:

1. the ability to adopt and sustain a role

2. the use of planning and preparation time

3. the style of questioning used

4. the review and evaluation of the drama activities.

Stage 1: a tutor teaching drama with primary pupils

The session began with a sense of anticipation and there being something out of the ordinary about to take place. After the tutor's introductory remarks, his entrance in role as a training officer for detectives was accepted seriously; pupils indicated their own change of role through simple body language (for example, formal attitudes, sitting up straight, serious facial expressions). Pupils also responded positively, and knowingly, to the opening greeting and implicit challenge of the prospective detectives' training course.

> *Teacher in role:* Welcome to this training course for detectives. I know you have all had invitations, and I know you have been highly recommended by your commanding officers back at your home police forces. So congratulations on being offered a place on this training course. But, I do have to tell you that this training course for expert detectives is not an easy training course. It is only the very best police officers that pass this training course and some of you may fail.

The series of games and tests enabled all pupils to participate and as the storytelling activities began the pupils were demonstrating a clear sense of their role as police officers. This development was regularly supported by the tutor's remarks in role as the training officer, for example 'as police officers I know you can be trusted', 'ladies and gentlemen' or more explicitly:

> *Teacher:* Imagine you are a police officer, and you are about to interview a witness who has just witnessed a road accident.

Here, the task was clearly defined as taking a witness' statement after a road accident, and the pupils incorporated a number of linguistic and paralinguistic techniques into their behaviour to reinforce their role-playing. Using mime to indicate note taking and the use of a tape recorder were two examples performed without self-consciousness. Subsequent extra roles (or roles within a role) were also taken on when police officers had to give accurate verbal reports to a demanding police sergeant, who in turn had to report to the bad-tempered station inspector, played by the tutor in role. This was undertaken with a sense of enthusiasm yet without undermining the formal and pressurised nature of the role-play interactions.

Further evidence of the pupils' ability to sustain their roles was demonstrated in their ability to instigate and pursue a spontaneous discussion on the nature of undercover work and the difficulty of recording information when assigned to these duties.

Not unsurprisingly, therefore, the pupils approached their preparation and planning for the alibis and interrogations seriously and intensely. Strict time limits and a fictional crime based on an act of vandalism to a local school aided this involvement. Once again those playing suspects were reminded that as police officers they were playing a role within a role; this did not dilute the feeling of excitement as alibis were first generated and then refined. Typical extracts would read:

A group with two suspects (S.1, S.2)

S.1:   Should we go to the cinema in Richmond?

S.2:   ... We went to Twickenham ... No, we went to Richmond, and we went over the bridge, and then we went to the cinema, and after that we went to Pizza Hut and got something to eat and went home.

S.1:   Yeah, so the cinema would probably take about two hours.

124

S.2:   Yeah.

A group with three suspects (S.3, S.4, S.5)

S.3:   Then what happened?

S.4:   Look, we went to the bus stop and got R70 to Richmond which cost us 30p each.

S.3:   So that's 60 ... er, 90p ... yeah.

S.5:   [*nods*] Yeah.

S.4:   So we'll say we got on and paid 90p out of the money your mum gave us.

S.5:   [*nods*] Yeah.

Pupils playing detectives were equally keen to sustain and develop their roles. It was interesting to note the intensity with which two mild-mannered girls (D.1 and D.2) questioned one of the above suspects (S.5):

D.1:   Were you anywhere near the window ... could you look out?

S.5:   No ... there was like ...

D.1:   Were you anywhere near the actual school?

S.5:   Er, no ...

D.2:   What did you actually do after you'd been to Pizza Hut?

S.5:   We went back to Dilip's house ...

D.2:   [*interrupting*] What did you do there?

S.5:   Well, we played a game, baseball, and painting ...

D.2:   [*interrupting*] And who won baseball?

S.5:   [*smiling*] I did.

D.2:   Right.

D.1:   [*interjecting*] Did you eat anything there?

S.5:   [*thinks*] ...

D.2:   [*continuing*] OK, what did you do after the painting?

S.5:	Went home.
D.2:	How did you go home?
S.5:	By bus.
D.2:	What bus?
S.5:	290.
D.1:	[*together*] What time was it ...
D.2:	[*together*] Did you go home or did Dilip go with you?
S.5:	No ... Danny ...
D.1:	[*together*] What time was it when you got back to your house?
D.2:	[*together*] Right, where was ... did you sit upstairs or downstairs?
S.5:	[*nervous*] We sat downstairs.
D.1:	What time was it when you got back to your house?
S.5:	Ten minutes past nine ... something like that.
D.1:	Did you pass the school on your way back?
S.5:	[*hesitates*] Yeah.
D.1:	Did you see anything there?
S.5:	No ... [*shakes head*] no ... I saw a lock broken there.
D.1:	Did you see anyone walking around it?
S.5:	No.
D.2:	And what time did you pass the school?
S.5:	Nine.

The fictional context not only enables pupils to experience a range of language uses and a sense of audience, but, as evidenced here, there is the opportunity to bring together thought and feeling; the emotional commitment given to the roles enables the pupils to develop an understanding of the power of language.

It is clear that when children are fully engaged in drama, emotionally, physically and intellectually, the language they use to express ideas reveals that their emotional engagement stimulates intellectual

growth. The intimate relationship between intellect and emotion is clearly seen in the expressive language identified ... the incidence of which was far greater than that found in other classroom contexts.
(Parsons *et al.* 1984, p.21)

When the next suspect enters the detectives are just as forceful, but the next suspect (S.4) is determined not to be pressurised:

D.2: Where were you between six and nine-thirty?

S.4: First ...

D.2: [*attempts interruption*] ...

S.4: [*leans forward*] Will you shut up and let me tell the story? [*leans back*] Right, I was with ... [*hesitates*]. First of all, Dilip phones me up ...

D.1: [*interrupts*] What time was it?

S.4: About ten to six. I went across the road ... to those ... to Joshua and Dilip, to buy Dilip a present.

D.2: Why are you buying him presents?

S.4: Because he'd invited us to his birthday party. I took the presents down to his house ...

D.2: Yeah.

S.4: ... and by the time I had got there it was three minutes to nine and Joshua and Dilip were there. We went inside, and he said we are going to Pizza Hut.

D.2: Are you sure that's right?

S.4: No, three minutes to six.

D.2: Yeah.

S.4: We got on the 290. Dilip paid 90p for all of us.

D.2: That's 30p each?

S.4: Yes, and we sat down ...

D.2: [*interrupts*] Upstairs or downstairs?

S.4: Downstairs ... because the 290 is a single decker bus. We arrived in Richmond. We went in Pizza Hut, and Dilip opened the presents in Pizza Hut.

Following the interrogations, pupils engaged in heated, but orderly, discussions between detectives and suspects where discrepancies were pointed out and disagreements were voiced.

Reflection, as it occurs in the drama and after role-playing has ceased, will often focus on fundamental issues embedded in the subject matter. With these Year 5 and 6 pupils, the emotional involvement in the drama stimulated discussion on the nature of evidence and the importance of recording information.

It was the pupils as detectives who requested the use of note pads and pencils rather than it being the suggestion of the teacher. Developments in police procedures were also highlighted by pupils still in role during the concluding discussion.

Finally, the use of the regular class teacher in role as commanding officer enabled the drama to finish in a ritualistic way through a passing out ceremony. Pupils were congratulated and received formal recognition for their contributions. Out of role, the pupils further revealed powers for reflective discussion and evidence that they recognised the benefits of drama as a learning medium. Outcomes identified by the pupils ranged from the philosophical concerning 'What is truth?' to the 'ability to ask questions' to the slightly perplexing 'solving household problems'. In response to a question on the benefits of the lesson one tutor-pupil interaction was:

Pupil: It lets you let your imagination ... put yourself in other people's position ...

Teacher: Is that good?

Pupil: Yes.

Teacher: Why?

Pupil: Because it's nice to know what other people's life-styles are ... and to work with other people.

Stage 2: drama with a PGCE group of primary students

Whilst attempting to retain the overall structure and focus of the material in Stage 1, the 'detectives project' when presented to PGCE students inevitably involved a number of significant differences. A simple transmission model of the tutor describing the activities as an example of good practice, perhaps with the aid of video material, was rejected. The philosophy of the course and the nature of arts education demanded a more experiential approach, the experience of practical drama has become an important aspect of the English PGCE course. In this respect, the notion of reflective practice can be seen in two dimensions; one being the professional orientation of the students as they prepare for a teaching career, whilst a second is concerned with their personal learning in drama. Therefore, reflective elements play a much more significant part at this stage of professional training; reflection on the teaching being demonstrated, on the learning being experienced and on teaching to be anticipated. Characteristically, practical sessions will often have lengthy preambles and significant periods of time will also be devoted to post-drama discussion. The 'detectives project' began with reference to an example of good practice cited by HMI in the Aspects of Primary Education series (DES, 1990). A school working on a topic on the police involved a group of Year 6 pupils in the making of a police station.

> Acting as police experts, the children used the computer to record the information received. They were aware of the conventions of interviews, imitating the real-life police who had visited the school. The children's knowledge and understanding of the work of the police were enlarged by their reading, research and role-play of police procedures. The drama activities motivated learning in a number of areas; careful observation and recording; a clear and economical use of oral and written language.
> (DES 1990, p.1)

Using the stimulus of a handout based on the HMI report and further information on the importance of inquiry skills, the tutor's aim was to offer a number of practical teaching and learning strategies to students for consideration and possible future use in their own teaching.

After the introduction to the unit of work, the tutor in role as a training officer established the context of a detectives' training school. Through a series of tests and games similar to those in Stage 1, the students were encouraged to enter the roles of trainee detectives. This period of introductory activity was extended further than was the case with the pupils in Stage 1. Two important reasons for this emerged. First, students did not adopt their acting roles as readily as their pupil counterparts; visual signals such as different body posture, changed facial expressions were not immediately incorporated into the students' behaviour, nor did tone of voice obviously change. There was interest and definite involvement, but little overt role-playing. Second, a wider repertoire of activities was used with the students in order to demonstrate the range of choices available to teachers who may need to work with a variety of classes in a variety of circumstances.

During the phase involving storytelling activities the students were, however, more demonstrably in role. Here, the task set was slightly more complex than in Stage 1 in that students were asked to review in role their past cases as police officers and to choose one case which involved clearly identified skills of observation. Using first person narrative these case histories were recounted to partners. The task demanded role-playing and narrative skills; students were able to sustain their roles as police officers whilst giving lengthy accounts of their particular crime. There were few interruptions from partners except for questions of clarification; in this way they were able to listen intently and to report accurately their colleagues' cases. It would appear that the student group were more at ease using verbal skills to adopt and sustain their roles as police officers, unlike the pupil group who found access to their roles through more physical routes.

The storytelling activities were further developed through the construction of a court scene where volunteer police officers had to report the details of a case they had heard but now under the added pressure of cross-examination. Here too the college-based development of the project allowed for the demands of students operating at a sophisticated level of personal language skill and intellectual ability but also attended to the professional concerns of students who wanted to experiment with various teaching strategies for different groups of children. This model of professional development eschews a simple apprenticeship style of training in favour of an approach which aims to encourage students to generate their own future content and range of teaching styles.

A further extension activity followed which sought to explore the possibilities of organising whole-class problem-solving exercises. The whole group were assigned to the investigation of a kidnapping mystery, and the atmosphere of a police incident room was replicated with victim's photograph and salient details posted on a flip chart for continual reference by the investigating officers. The distribution of information was controlled by the tutor in role as a chief inspector, outside the actual investigation but needing speedy results. The whole group experienced processes of investigation, mixed groupings, spontaneous and hypothesising talk, deductive reasoning, leadership roles, consensual and co-operative talk, decision making, whilst remaining firmly in role as trainee detectives. The group successfully solved the kidnapping mystery and were given further opportunity to reflect on the development of their roles and the skills afforded by this type of activity.

Consequently, during the main phase of the project, namely the alibis section, students were able to demonstrate strong commitment to the drama in general and their own roles in particular. The crime and the investigation were introduced in a similar fashion to that used with pupils at Stage 1, although details differed. The training officer's outline of the crime differed slightly:

> *Teacher in role:* Wilson's, the well known electrical retailers, was broken into last night and £5,000 worth of equipment was stolen ... You are investigating this crime. Suspects were seen at the back of Wilson's between the hours of eight o'clock and midnight. You as the detectives leading this case have invited three suspects into the police station to undergo an interview; let's not call it an interrogation ... yet.

Students as suspects and as detectives received further advice and guidance in separate groups. Very strong similarities now emerged between the working processes of the PGCE students and Year 6 pupils. Both groups could be characterised by their animated and energetic approach to their preparation. During briefing both groups were anxious to get on with their preparations. On viewing the video material it was interesting to note three students playing suspects unable to stop rehearsing and refining their alibi during the tutor's further guidance. They were entirely focussed on getting details correct. Therefore, student discussion on the use of planning and rehearsal time which included details of group organisation and leadership roles, patterns of work, individual's feelings and enthusiasms, revealed insights into the way pupils also learn during these phases of drama work. Details of the actual preparatory talk also exposed striking similarities between the student groups and the pupil groups. For example, two student suspects (S.1 and S.2) begin to construct their alibi in this way:

S.1:   ... video?

S.2:   *Silence of the Lambs* have you seen that?

S.1:   *Silence of the Lambs?*

S.2:   *Yeah.*

S.1:   We went to the cinema at ...?

S.2:   It started at ... what time ... eight o'clock.

S.1:	Where? At … Hounslow?
S.2:	There isn't a cinema in Hounslow.
S.1:	In Staines.
S.2:	In Staines … I've never been there.
S.1:	Slough.
S.2:	Have you been to Richmond?
S.1:	Yes.
S.2:	Right.
S.1:	We were at Richmond cinema.
S.2:	What time did it start?
S.1:	The film started at … eight.
S.2:	Eight?
S.1:	[*nods*] Eight o'clock.
S.2:	What are … what did we have to eat?
S.1:	I had popcorn.
S.2:	Yes.
S.1:	What did you have?
S.2:	Popcorn.
S.1:	Right, we had popcorn.
S.2:	Anything to drink …?

However, the students in role as detectives (D.1 and D.2) were able to make more explicit reference to the actual style of questioning they were about to adopt. In this respect not only did students require less guidance in terms of the range of interview techniques but they also gave as much attention to the style of delivery as they did to the content of questions. For example:

D.1:	We can have a sort of fairly laid back type of approach, but …
D.2:	Yeah.
D.1:	… but nasty.

D.2:	Yeah, when they start getting a bit nervous sort of go around them.
D.1:	Yeah, reiterate the questions we've already said. What questions are we going to ask them?
D.2:	Well, exactly where they were, what they were doing and also ...
D.1:	... who they were with.

This sophistication in terms of planned approaches to paralinguistic techniques can be clearly discerned in the actual interviews that followed. Tone of voice, gestures and facial signals, physical proximity and movement around the suspects were used to far greater effect. The content of the interchanges was not strikingly different from that found in the pupils' work, but the tone was far more intimidating. For example, this extract shows both detectives in the previous extract interviewing each of two suspects (S.3 and S.4).

D.2:	Take a seat.
D.1:	Would you like to state your name and occupation?
S.3:	My name is Kirsty Black, I'm 21, and, er, I'm a student.
D.1:	A student, right.
D.2:	What do you study?
S.3:	Er, I'm training to be a teacher.
D.1:	A teacher ... so a responsible post.
S.3:	[nods]
D.1:	So this could have an effect on whether you become a teacher or not?
S.3:	Yes.
D.1:	Right.
D.2:	OK. Can you tell me exactly what you were doing last night at eight o'clock?
S.3:	Eight o'clock ... I was probably sitting in the cinema.

The second suspect has similar treatment ...

D.2:	Take a seat. What's your name?

S.4:	Gemma Hurst.
D.1:	And your age?
S.4:	24.
D.1:	And your occupation?
S.4:	Student.
D.1:	Of what?
S.4:	PGCE.
D.1:	PGCE. What's that?
S.4:	Postgraduate Certificate of Education.
D.1:	So what are you training to be, are you training to be something?
S.4:	Training to be a teacher.
D.1:	OK, right.
D.2:	Another teacher ... respectable teachers. Can you tell me, Gemma please, what you was doing last night at eight o'clock?
S.4:	Well, I met Kirsty at the cinema at about half-seven so at eight o'clock we had gone in to the ...
D.2:	[*interrupts*] Oh, you met Kirsty at the cinema, did you? At what time was that?
S.4:	At half past seven.
D.2:	Interesting, very interesting.
S.4:	We were in the cinema by eight.
D.1:	And what did you go to see?
S.4:	*Silence of the Lambs.*
D.1:	OK, how long were you in the cinema?

Later they get even more devious ...

D.1:	So you left before the end of the film?
S.4:	No.
D.1:	You didn't?

S.4:	We watched the end of the film.
D.1:	You watched the end of the film?
S.4:	[*nods*] Yeah.
D.1:	Did you enjoy the film?
S.4:	Yep.
D.2:	Kirsty said her boyfriend picked her up at the end of the film in his sports car.
S.4:	No, no. We went for a pizza after ...
D.2:	[*interrupts*] Oh, a pizza. After all the popcorn you had a pizza?
S.4:	Yeah.
D.1:	What kind of pizza?
S.4:	A cheese supreme. Large.

The student groups' review and assessment of the alibis and the questioning procedures adopted produced similar disagreements to those of the pupils. However, at this stage it was noticeable that the sense of role-play was overtaken by a battle of wits between students not so much as suspects and detectives but purely as colleagues participating in an enjoyable intellectual activity. Once again the reflective discussion stimulated by the drama tended towards broad issues of social justice and the advisability of doing this work with pupils who may have domestic circumstances influenced by a background of criminal activity. This philosophical debate was also displayed at Stage 1 to a lesser degree and related more clearly to TV programmes, but the general phenomenon has been cited by drama practitioners as an important outcome for role-play activity:

> Reflection as it occurs during, and particularly after, the drama is over usually focuses on the fundamental issues of mankind. Such discussions make a valuable contribution to moral and values education. (Parsons *et al.* 1984, p.21)

Further consideration was also given to the teaching and learning of the project. The whole unit of work was formally reviewed making explicit the rationale, planning, organisation, content and intended outcomes. Collaborative role-play, as described here, was intended to provide a secure and enjoyable learning context in which children and students can draw on what they already know – rudimentary detection and police work as popularly portrayed on television, for example – and in which they can be encouraged and gently challenged to articulate questions, answers and narrative accounts with fluency and with appropriate disinterest and detachment.

Using more traditional lecturing strategies some potential learning outcomes were outlined, for example:

1. attentive listening – perhaps enhanced through note taking – and the active identification of salient narrative features

2. lucid description in which the ordering of events and the rehearsal of coherence and sequence will play a key part – and where, again, note taking and possibly the use of flow diagrams would be useful aids

3. the preparation of pertinent questions which seek elaboration and clarification – best exemplified in the 'alibis' section

4. awareness of and sensitivity to audience and interlocutor.

At this stage student reaction focussed on practical details and the variations that would be both possible and necessary for different groups in different circumstances. Here, more explicit professional concerns which were tackled indicated three levels of professional learning. First, at a technical level, students are keen to note the planning framework used and to reassure themselves of the content, progression and learning potential of the material. In effect they begin their lesson planning.

Second, students are expected to reflect on why certain actions were taken and strategies used. Speculation about institutional and situational variations is important so that students begin to appreciate the philosophical, social and psychological constraints that teachers must work with. They apply both personal and established theories to the choices presented to them. For example, the choice of two girls to play the role of detectives may not simply be an unconsidered action but a calculated decision.

Third, reflection itself introduces moral and ethical issues which present students with professional dilemmas. Some teachers may have ethical concerns when dealing with this type of content area especially considering some of the domestic circumstances of children in our schools. This level of reflection will cause teachers to adopt a personal stance towards the ideological aspects of teaching in general.

Student evaluation of this style of professional training and the principle of active involvement in drama as part of this professional preparation is the focus of Stage 3 of this case study.

Stage 3: an evaluative discussion with PGCE students

'Everyone was really into it.'

Reflection has been a key element in each of the drama sessions and, at the end of their short course, PGCE primary students were invited to view a 'rough cut' video of their work and to evaluate the programme. This session was, itself, video-recorded and, in this section, attention will be drawn to illuminative features of students' discussion, particularly regarding their own emergent professional voices.

The evaluation session was led by a tutor who welcomed the group to the viewing room and gave an introduction, drawing attention to the aims of the 'detectives' programme in relation to the development of enquiry skills. Prior to the screening students were given a list of points which it was felt would be useful to inform their viewing and for subsequent discussion. These points were given some preliminary gloss and were directed towards:

1. the quality of the video recording

2. the personal level of enjoyment and involvement experienced by students throughout the programme

3. the potential value of 'detectives' as a programme within a school environment

4. the extent to which participation in a drama session is useful in preparation for teaching

5. aspects of the programme needing modification or change.

The screening of the video was then followed by some lively general discussion. Student enjoyment was very evident as they watched themselves at work, and the video received a warm response. One student attracted the approval of the group as a whole when concluding preliminary discussion following the viewing:

Student: It showed that everyone was on task and really involved in what they were doing. A lot of the time when the video was panning people were obviously talking about the actual thing they were doing. Everyone was really into it.

Students were then divided into smaller groups with the task of reflecting upon the programme. The group given attention here was made up of eight students — six women and two men — and the tutor, Robert Catt. A selected transcript from the discussion is provided with additional commentary.

The group discussion was fluent and informal with a good deal of laughter and simultaneous speech. Even with the evidence of some skilfully produced videos it is often difficult to differentiate between speakers, and there is much shared agreement. The discussion is dominated by four speakers — and Mark, in particular — with two women students participating hardly at all. A technical transcription would be dense but some attempt is made here to convey the speed and excitement of talk aimed, generally, at the construction of shared meanings and characterised by what Coates (1994) refers to as 'No gap, lots of overlap'. Such overlap is indicated through '{' and speakers' lines are indented to indicate the absence of gaps in turn-taking.

During the early part of the discussion consensus is quickly achieved regarding the value of drama in the primary curriculum and the developmental potential in 'detectives'.

From some excited agreement, however, two concerns tentatively emerge. One regards role-play and, although the students seem to agree that they 'slipped into' role with ease, it is felt that pupils would need much more preparation through drama games. The second indicates that 'detectives', as a theme, might be remote from pupil experience and rather limiting. It is at this point that Mark begins to take a leading role in the discussion:

Mark: You have one session and you want to do a certain amount and there's nothing in that session which says this is as far as you can go ... whether it's drama or anything ... You get a starting point ... you can always develop it and that ... rather than doing it in one session you could develop it for a whole year ... or a whole term ... and develop it in which-ever direction you wanted.

Mark is clearly excited by the programme (and, in the video, he clearly enjoys his role-play) in which he can spot clear developmental potential. To an extent his enthusiasm is infectious and is certainly

---

a catalyst for some subsequently dense and excited exchange. It is, however, unfortunate that his confident approach – evident in the hyperbole of 'a whole year' – is insensitive to the gender dynamic of the group and tends to block out the more tentative reflections of at least three other students.

It is with some awareness of the need to draw in a more representative range of voices that the tutor, Robert Catt (RC), quickly reminds students of the need to consider the value of the programme in relation to their own personal and professional development. This period within the discussion will now be examined in some detail.

RC: I wouldn't mind dwelling on this for you at your level.

Mark: {Right.

RC: {What about voice in terms of you as a speaker? I mean something that I'm very interested in terms of teaching is in providing youngsters with opportunities to become competent speakers in a range of repertoire.

Mark: {Right.

RC: {It's not just children is it? [sympathetic laughter] I mean as adults ... I mean I go to meetings, like this, and I want to say something but I don't. I don't know why ... because I feel it's going to come out backwards or something. [laughter] I'm reluctant and I suspect that many people are like that. Does a session involving simulation and role-play like detectives ... Does that help in a way?

Liz: {Yes ...

Sarah: {Yes, only it makes you realise you could do with an awful lot more of it.

Mark: Well I ... I think it's noticeable in our group when you watch something like that where everyone's speaking and everyone's getting involved because generally in most of the things ... then it would be like three people who talk in all our lectures. [laughter] I mean I know I'm one of them [laughter] and Don usually has a word and then someone else will have a word but generally everyone else has got loads of opinions and nobody actually ... says ... They won't voice them. But in a session like that { they all ...

Liz:	{When … whenyou'reinarole … Whenit's … I mean, when it's not actually { you speaking you're …
Denise:	{Speaking it's much easier.
RC:	Why … why is it easier?
Liz:	You don't take responsibility …
Denise:	It's not you. In a sense it's someone else.
Beth:	I don't agree … I found that more stressful than … than { normally …
Mark:	{ But you get … But people spoke a lot more on there in front of everyone else … I mean … it's much more { info …
Sarah:	{ You're focussed into a task aren't you? You know you've got a task … and it's fair and … straightforward, and if you're focussed on that somehow it's easier. [*muttered agreement from several students*]
Mark:	Generally as a group … I don't know what other groups are like but there's not really much input in anyway …
Liz:	Well, there's no pressure in drama that what you say is going to be wrong … you know, or is going to be accepted … What you say is fine … I mean a lot of lectures you … you're worried { about …
Denise:	{ getting it { wrong …
Liz:	{ … does it sound ridiculous? Probably what you're thinking is right. It generally is when the answer comes out or when somebody's opinion is expressed.
Beth:	[*oppositional*] But then you didn't find that that situation was actually stressful itself? That we were supposed to be the top detectives or we were supposed to know something and the fact that { we didn't…?
Liz:	{ But none of us did.
Mark:	{ No. [*emphatic*] No because it was a role-play. { I think …
Beth:	[*defensive*] { Well that's how I found it …
Don:	[*forceful*] It was only stressful because the camera was there.

Sarah: Also I find a ... you know ... a lot of lectures stressful because I'm aware I'm in a classroom. When we're doing drama it doesn't feel so much like we're in a classroom. It feels like something ... different. We're not all sitting ... we're not all static ... you know, we're not all just sort of in a circle like we are here we [*murmurs of agreement*] { get ...

Liz: { No [*agreeing*]

Sarah: ... up and do other things which ... [*pause*]

RC: [*to Sarah*] I don't want to suggest that that's a problem but, is it something which has a history? I mean have you always { found ...

Sarah: { Yeah.

RC: ... it in a way ... not difficult, but { awkward to ...?

Sarah: { Yeah ... yeah ... because it feels less like a classroom I find it a lot easier ... more ... [*long hesitation*]

Denise: [*To Sarah – whispering*] Appealing?

Sarah: Yeah. [*pause*]

RC: [*to Beth – encouraging*] You don't. Tell us. Just explain a little bit.

Beth: Well, no. I'm just saying in that situation, I find it more stressful than normally ... than ... Because we were supposed to be the experts that I was more worried about if I'd said something that I'd got it wrong that ... Whereas in a normal classroom situation if I'd said something and it was wrong well it was my opinion. It ... you know it didn't really matter. [*pause*]

RC: So you identified very heavily with the role. [*loud group laughter*] Quite clearly.

Beth: [*laughing*] { Well. I suppose so. [*laughter*]

Mark: { ... thought you'd be drummed out of the force if you weren't careful.

Beth: [*laughing*] Well, it was ... it was something like that.

Liz: Maybe if it was a subject which was a bit more familiar, that you knew more about, rather than detectives ... I mean, I was a little bit worried at the start of it but once I got into it I was all right.

Beth: I mean, silly little things like when we had to go round and say what force we were in ... Like, I mean, I suddenly thought I don't know any police forces. [*laughter*]

RC: You coped with it very well ... I mean there was no difficulty ...no visible difficulty.

As a text this transcript has a good deal of intrinsic potential: the dominant length of Mark's turns; the frequent and generally supportive overlap between Sarah, Liz and Denise; the influence of contextual murmur and laughter; Beth's bravely persistent insistence of the difficulty she encountered within the drama programme. In a sense this opens that 'window' to which we referred earlier to reveal something of the texture of our work in HE. In this respect the transcript is indicative of those oppositional voices which frequently and quite rightly arise in student seminars. Beth is resisting the 'positioning' pressure of the discourse and provides a salutary reminder of the understandable difficulty which many children will experience in role-play. This is a point which the tutor will later explore. Here, however, the intention of this brief commentary is to identify those evaluative features indicative of the importance of drama in HE. In this respect the text speaks almost for itself. Mark points out that, remarkably, all students seem to have been actively involved in the programme whereas, in conventional lectures, 'it would be like three people who talk'. Putting aside for a moment the irony that, even given his disclaimer − 'I know I'm one of them' − Mark seems oblivious to his dominance, there is evident potential in role-play for active learning, as Liz paradoxically suggests, 'when it's not actually you speaking'.

Towards the end of subsequent discussion the students are vocal regarding the importance of opportunities such as these which, they claim, would make a 'major contribution' to their course. Beth's opposition and, indeed, the absence of two other student voices, must, however, be considered. To an extent Beth reverses the views of Liz and Sarah that voice through role is easier. At first her objection that she feels under stress in the role of expert seems simply curious especially as, when in 'a normal classroom situation', a 'wrong' answer would merely be her 'opinion'. It is unfortunate that Mark's clever quip tends to distract (intentionally?) from the impact of her opposition. Her subsequent reference to 'silly little things', however, is powerfully suggestive of the importance of providing a safe structure within which role-play can take place. Liz is particularly supportive of Beth; she identifies with her initial anxieties but is pleasantly reassuring.

Remarkable in the students' informal evaluation of the course as a whole are their comments about the paucity of opportunity for the development of a voice in discussion both at undergraduate and postgraduate levels. There was overwhelming demand for more work involving simulation and role-play.

Stage 4: a PGCE student teaching drama on final TP

The final stage of the case study is intended to illustrate how one student from the PGCE group developed the 'detectives project' whilst undertaking his final teaching practice. He successfully organised the material into three teaching sessions to coincide with his allocation of 'hall time'. The third and final lesson was recorded on video tape and this consisted in the main of the alibis activity.

First, it should be noted that the student had confidence in the feasibility of the material and its potential with his particular class of Year 6 pupils. It was clear from the outset that the previous two lessons had motivated the class, and pupils quickly adopted their roles as police officers. An important feature of the whole lesson was the attention given by the student to aspects of class management and control. Organisational aspects such as grouping, use of space, movement around the room, allocations of time, were all clearly monitored and controlled by the student. Sometimes this was demonstrably part of the student's and pupils' role-playing but at other times it was a necessary teaching strategy which the student did not hesitate to use.

Throughout, the basic framework of the college-based session was retained by the student but it was invested with increased formality. The safety of the workshop and experimental atmosphere of college was recognised and the rigours of school practice fully appreciated in the adaptations incorporated into the student's version of the 'detectives' project. In role as the training officer he spoke with a clipped tone, stood to attention, paced purposefully using a no-nonsense form of introduction:

> *Student teacher:* Good afternoon everyone ... Glad to see everyone fit and well. A good night's sleep? [*nods from pupils*] First, I want to

say congratulations on getting so far in the course. A lot of policemen being sent here would have dropped out by now. You've done very very well. Obviously your station commanders were right to send you here. I'm very impressed.

After recapping the tests of observation and exercises that required deductive thinking, he went on to introduce the alibis activity thus:

> *Student teacher*: Today, I am going to check and see how good your questioning technique is. You all know how very important it is for a detective to ask the right questions and find out if a suspect is lying or not.

Links with on-going topic work were also made through the use of a fictional robbery of rare stamps from the British Museum. Also, unlike the college-based session, here the student rehearsed with the whole class the style and content of the forthcoming interviews. He invited suggestions for possible questions and modelled different styles of questioning. This type of teaching strategy, discussed during the post-drama reflective discussion in college, was evidently noted by this particular student and might be seen as an example of reflection-on-action, although there were missed opportunities where the quality of pupils' interaction could have been improved. The student's ability to react to unplanned events, to reflect-in-action (Schön 1987), was evidenced in his response to pupils' questions:

Pupil 1: How can you think of questions without knowing the alibi?

Teacher: As experienced detectives I would have thought that was obvious.

And again:

Pupil 2: Are we allowed to shout at them?

Teacher: You have to interview them as you would normally do at your station. When you have a suspect at your station, follow the same rules. So obviously ... I don't know what you do behind closed doors ... but obviously excessive shouting and the use of any kind of violence will not be accepted.

Grouping was firmly controlled by the student (although, by now, not clearly in role as the training officer); the pairing of certain pupils and the allocation of space appeared to be of more concern to him than the quality of role-playing. In this respect the alibis activity, although accomplished in an effective manner, did not exploit the full potential of the language possibilities of the drama activities. When compared to Stages 1 and 2 of the case study the content of the alibis displayed some similarities, for example, eating pizza, cost of cinema tickets, details of journeys, but the interchanges between detectives and suspects (represented here by D.1 and S.2, respectively) did not display dramatic qualities in the style of questioning.

D.1: What did you eat?

S.2: I can't remember because I wasn't eating because I wasn't hungry.

D.1: Right, what your friends eating then?

S.2: I was reading a newspaper, I don't know.

D.1: And ... em ... if you looked out the window did you see ... like ... museum things?

S.2: [*shakes head*] No.

D.1: Any stamps on the floor?

S.2: No.

D.1: Did your parents come back? Did your friend's parents come back?

S.2: Ten-thirty.

D.1: And what time did you go ... bed?

S.4: I stayed at her house, and ... like ... we had to go to bed at twelve o'clock.

In assessing the alibis, control was once again very much to the forefront of the student's thinking in that suspects and detectives were not encouraged to regroup in order to review the stories and discrepancies. This was handled through a plenary discussion controlled by the student. Nor at this stage were pupils encouraged to remain in role as police officers.

Nevertheless, an effective piece of teaching and learning was achieved. Pupils' learning tended to reside in the sphere of social skills and personal development. Whereas the student demonstrated a growing awareness of his own ability to manage the class in practical group work as well as showing further insight into the teaching of drama to Key Stage 2 pupils. The final section of this chapter will attempt to summarise and identify significant aspects of this professional learning.

(iv)

Conclusion

Reflective practice

This case study has attempted to illustrate an example of reflective practice whereby tutors and students focus on their own teaching and learning experiences in order to gain insights into their professional development. A model of training founded on technical-rational principles where students learn and practise set procedures in the laboratory atmosphere of college has been rejected because it underestimates the complexity and unpredictability of teaching in schools.

> The assumption here is that each situation will be similar enough to a routine model to apply the predetermined and practised technical procedures. However, when the 'real' situation involves people, then every situation becomes unique and many will fail to yield to the pre-learnt repertoire.
> (Fish 1988, p.26)

Teaching in general is seen as a more creative and artistic process that requires technical skill but much more besides, not least the need to improvise and to 'think on one's feet'.

For this theoretical foundation we depend much on Schön's explanation of 'reflection-in-action' (Schön 1987). Schön's distinction between reflection-on-action and reflection-in-action puts particular emphasis on the phrase 'in action' thus highlighting the experiential possibilities of professional preparation (Russell 1989). Student teachers are encouraged to reflect on events from their own teaching and the teaching of others and are encouraged to generate questions, to problematise the situation and to develop further possibilities. Central to much of this discourse is the notion of 'practical knowledge'. The ability to see teaching as a practical activity that is essentially problematic is a distinguishing characteristic of the reflective practitioner.

Practice is therefore at the heart of the enterprise; at different times the focus of ITE will range from the practice of experienced teachers to the simulated experiences of workshop activity and micro-teaching to the actual teaching and learning of students. The settings will undergo corresponding shifts between college and school and between the real and the simulated.

The emerging partnerships between schools and colleges would seem to indicate a positive development in the preparation of teachers who are aware of the links between theory and practice.

Yet, this is not without difficulties in that those who advocate school-based training presuppose that relevant and meaningful opportunities for practice do exist in all our schools.

Curriculum provision in the arts

The range of provision in primary schools for all subjects, and the arts in particular, is not consistent. It is a view held by those who work and research in primary schools that time given to the arts has diminished and is in danger of further reductions if there is not careful attention given to the notion of overall balance in the curriculum. (Dearing 1993; HMI 1990; Taylor and Andrews 1993). Not that there is dispute concerning the general principle of including the arts in a broadly based curriculum but in times of economic constraint and political pressure other priorities assume greater importance.

> The importance of the arts has been acknowledged but rarely given detailed attention. In practice the arts have often been marginalised in schools by an assumption that they are less relevant to contemporary priorities than technological or scientific education.
> (NCC 1990, p.7)

Indeed, it is significant to note that the once chairman of the NCC, David Pascall, considered it necessary during his final period in office to make the case for the arts:

> The case for the importance of the cultural dimension and the civilising power of the arts for all our children needs to be put. I should like today to discuss the intellectual rationale for a balanced and broadly based curriculum in which the cultural dimension in general and the arts in particular have their crucial place.
> (Pascall 1992, p.3)

In preparing the young for adult life it is usual to find a utilitarian argument that is apt to stress the scientific, mathematical and technological subjects. Yet, for the majority of citizens, it is true to say that their everyday lives are as much concerned with arts-related activities as with the purely vocational. Watching TV dramas, listening to popular music, buying fashionable clothes, dancing at family celebrations and discos are for many individuals the 'real stuff' of adult life.

In terms of ITE, there is an obvious contradiction emerging if schools are to be the leading partners in training future teachers of the arts when in reality the opportunities for experiencing the arts in schools is diminishing.

Teachers and the arts

It is clear from research that one of the major reasons for the lack of consistent and widespread good practice in the teaching of the arts is the perceived lack of confidence and expertise by teachers themselves. How the transfer of pre-service training from colleges to schools will begin to address this problem is not immediately clear. Beginning teachers are not going to find a large reservoir of arts education expertise in our schools, although this is not to underestimate the wealth of exciting projects that are undertaken by committed teachers. However, it is clear that arts education is not approached by the vast majority of primary teachers with the same degree of knowledge, skill and confident understanding as other areas of the curriculum. Regular surveys by HMI, together with their specialist findings in the Aspects of Primary Education series (DES 1990 etc.) cite evidence of disappointing provision for the arts in general and dance and drama in particular.

> Teachers frequently expressed the view that they lacked the confidence and expertise to provide adequate arts experiences for their pupils. As a result, a detailed analysis of lessons observed in art, music, dance and drama was subsequently carried out, and confirmed the impression that in many schools the provision of experiences in these areas of the curriculum left much to be desired.
> (Cleave and Sharp 1986, p.3)

Therefore, for those concerned with the arts in ITE there are a number of uncomfortable questions to address which are given added poignancy by the development of school-centred training. In what ways can the case for the arts in the curriculum be best

148

formulated? And how are beginning teachers effectively trained to become knowledgeable, confident and willing teachers of the arts? It is the exposure of this dual concern for personal arts experience for student primary teachers and for their empowering professional preparation in the arts that has been the aim of this case study.

References

Arts Council of Great Britain (1992) *Drama in schools: Arts Council guidance on drama education.* London: Arts Council of Great Britain.
Cleave, R. and Sharp, S. (1986) *The arts: preparation to teach.* London: NFER.
Coates, E. (1994) 'No gaps, lots of overlap: turn-taking, patterns in the talk of women friends', in Graddol, D., Maybin, J. and Stiever, B. (Eds) *Researching language and literacy in social contexts.* Avon: Open University Press, pp.177–92.
Dearing, R. (1993) *The National Curriculum and its assessment.* London: SCAA.
DES (1989) *Drama from 5 to 16 (Curriculum Matters 17)* (HMI Series) London: HMSO.
DES (1990) *Aspects of primary education: the teaching and learning of drama.* London: HMSO.
Fish, D. (1988) *Turning teaching into learning.* London: West London Press.
Groundwater-Smith, S. (1984) 'The portrayal of schooling and the literature of fact', *Curriculum Perspectives,* 4 (2), pp.1–6.
Hornbrook, D. (1991) *Education in drama: casting the dramatic curriculum.* London: Falmer Press.
NCC Arts in Schools Project (1990) *The arts 5–16: a curriculum framework.* Essex: Oliver and Boyd.
NCC (1991) *Drama in the National Curriculum.* London: NCC (poster)
Neelands, J. (1992) *Learning through imagined experience.* London: Hodder and Stoughton.
Parsons, B., Schaffner, M., Little, G. and Felton, H. (1984) *Drama, language and learning.* Tasmania: National Association for Drama in Education.
Pascall, D. (1992) *The cultural dimension in education.* London: Speech at Royal Society of Arts.
Russell, T. (1989) 'Documenting reflection-in-action in the classroom: searching for appropriate methods', *Qualitative Studies in Education,* 2 (4), pp.275–84.
Schön, D.A. (1987) *Educating the reflective practitioner.* London: Jossey Bass.
Taylor, R. and Andrews, G. (1993) *The arts in the primary school.* London: Falmer Press.
Woolland, B. (1993) *The teaching of drama in the primary school.* Essex: Longman.
Zuber-Skerritt, O. (1992) *Professional development in higher education.* London: Kogan Page.

Part 3

Quality in Tutors' Educational Practice:
The Particular and the General

CHAPTER 8

Tutors' Educational Practices: A Critical Overview

Introduction

This chapter offers an editor's cross-case interpretation (or interpretative survey) of the studies presented in Part 2 above. It should be noted that this work is explored from a reflective practitioner standpoint. In so doing it follows the work of Schön (1987) and is based on the ideas of Stenhouse (1980, 1982 and 1985) on case study and of Atkinson and Delamont (1986) who argue for comparative analyses across studies. This analysis can develop the studies into a more general framework by characterising features, problems and issues common to a range of different concrete settings. Atkinson and Delamont talk of analysis where I would wish to speak of interpretation, but the principles are the same. Interpretation here is in the tradition of historical and literary interpretation as opposed to scientific classification and analysis (see Grundy 1987).

By means of an interpretative survey, then, this chapter focusses upon significant aspects of these tutors' roles as they emerge through the practice reported. It seeks to bring up to tutors' studies a range of theoretical perspectives including those from writing on professional development in in-service teacher education and to offer a critical overview by seeking to explore, clarify and consider the tutors' intentions, expertise, activities and achievements. The following chapter focusses in detail on tutors' practices in facilitating students' professional development through practical discourse. This emerges sharply from the studies as a central thrust of the current work in ITE of an education tutor, and there are also interesting perspectives on aspects of this from a range of formal writings.

152

The final chapter, then, makes suggestions and a proposal which might enable tutors to work to clarify further, understand better and open to public scrutiny, their theory and practice; and all readers to harness the insights offered in the crucial debates that must take place in the mid-1990s about the shape of tutors' future contributions to ITE.

In order to provide a clear critical overview, this chapter is divided into five parts. The first section explains the intentions of the cross-case study and the methods used; the second looks at tutors' aims and intentions in working with students and their underlying values and beliefs; the third looks at tutors' knowledge, qualities and attributes which are drawn upon in work with students; and the fourth section looks at tutors' main activities as they work with students from within an education department. The fifth and final section offers a brief critical overview. In each of these sections are provided: key definitions and consideration of any relevant technical language; explorations of some theoretical dimensions; practical examples drawn from the studies; and an attempt to highlight significant values, beliefs and theories-in-use illustrated in the ways tutors present their studies and present themselves and their interactions with students.

(i)

Exploring the tutors' studies

This section indicates how the studies were explored and why particular theoretical approaches were used to enlighten them. It explains the intentions of the interpretative survey, the processes used, the personal theories underpinning the survey's design, as well as the procedures adopted to try to widen and further validate the interpretation offered.

Intentions

In exploring the tutors' studies with the intention of illuminating their work, I am attempting to achieve:

> the careful confrontation of principles with cases, of general rules
> with concrete documented events — a dialectic of the general with

the particular in which the limits of the former and the boundaries
of the latter are explored.
(Shulman, quoted in Stones 1992, p.309)

It should be noted that I am therefore seeking to operate exactly in
the way that tutors seek to work with their students. I am exploring
some specific practical examples of *tutors'* craft knowledge, know-
how, expertise and their associated personal theories, values and
beliefs. And I am trying to bring this into sharply focussed relationship with systematic theory culled from a range of sources, the
choice of which is explained below. I thus seek to make a 'properly
critical study of educational practice' (Kelly 1993, p.133). But I do
not share what I detect may be Shulman's emphasis on starting with
the principles and seeking to refine general rules. My interest is in
starting with, and seeking to understand, tutors' practices. Such
work might also contribute in a small way to the refinement of
specific practice and to broader discussions about ITE.

The value-base from which I seek to work is shaped by a quartet
of firm (but never final) commitments which I have developed from
small-scale but systematic theoretical and practical investigations of
my own practice in ITE over many years, and which owe nothing
at all to band-waggons and fluctuating fashions. These four commitments are as follows:

1. I believe still that Curriculum Studies offers the best approach
   to the study of education (including teacher education) because
   it seeks to place practice at the centre of its work and to draw
   theory from a broad range of relevant *practice-oriented* disciplines to enlighten it. (See below for a detailed exploration of
   this.) I nevertheless recognise that in contradistinction to this
   some people believe that the application of theory from a particular scientific (theoretically oriented) domain like psychology
   ought to give students a clearer knowledge-base from which to
   work (see, for example, Stones 1992).

2. I am persuaded that reflective practice offers the best means
   of preparing student teachers, and refining and improving
   practice in teaching, because it requires a holistic approach to
   education and does justice to the complexity of teaching and
   learning, although I am aware that its traditions, concepts and
   vocabulary are still emerging. I recognise, however, that others
   argue that reflective practice does not offer student teachers the
   assurance of certainty which they argue is needed by novice pro-

154

fessionals as a basis for their work in the classroom (see, for example, Gilroy 1993; Tickle 1993).

3. I believe that ITE is an enterprise which belongs in HE, and though I recognise that the present government is committed to removing it from that arena, I believe that the debate about this must be kept open.

4. I hold that only by exploring fully the current HE contribution to ITE and trying to capture and understand a broad range of examples of tutors' current work can we provide a proper base for considering the value of this work and ultimately for deciding the best future shape of teacher preparation. (Of course, *this* publication can claim to make only a very small contribution in this direction.)

Processes

I have adopted three procedures in attempting this cross-case study. First, I scrutinised the studies in an open-ended way for views that emerged. In listing these I found that most of the issues concerned the use of a range of experiential learning and the consequent attempt to enhance students' educational understandings by means of practical discourse (although not all studies used these terms).

The rest of my list, culled from an open-minded (but still subjective) scrutiny of the studies, turned out to consist of qualities, knowledge and attributes which the writers considered specific to education tutors and their work with student teachers. These I have come to see as part of the knowledge-base upon which a tutor works and as a result they appear as part of the third section of this chapter. Most of the studies focus on the processes tutors use. They do not *centre* on the details of key issues of ITE that are also important to students' understanding of their wider professional role (for example, the aims of education; specific perspectives on teaching and learning, assessment and appraisal; school management; and the education system and the law). To do justice to this would demand another publication.

Readers can, of course, try the exercise of re-reading the studies in Part 2 for emerging issues, before reading the rest of this chapter and then compare their findings with my own.

Second, informed by the reading of a range of literature, I sought emerging categories which would enable me to explore, across the studies, the tutors' role in facilitating students' professional learning.

I also recognised the need to attempt to highlight their (usually tacit) 'values, strategies and underlying assumptions' as they emerged from their writing (their *espoused theories* of action used to explain and justify behaviour) and to deduce the (possibly incongruent) theories implicit in their patterns of spontaneous behaviour (their *theories-in-use*) (see Schön 1987, pp.255–6). To tutors' specific descriptions of their practice, offered in their own voices, I have brought up theoretical perspectives from literature.

Of course, I recognise that the selection of these categories is temporary, arbitrary and that they overlap. And I am aware that my identification of quotations from tutors' studies, my use of them, my deductions about tutors' theories, and my choice of related literature, are entirely subjective. Persuaded by arguments well put by Grundy that 'confidence in an interpretation depends upon agreement with others that such an interpretation is reasonable' (Grundy 1987, p.14), I also asked the writers of the studies to participate in a day workshop session (which was video-ed) to discuss their aims, their espoused theories-of-action as education tutors working with student teachers, to investigate their actual theories-in-use, to comment upon and discuss my categories and to consider their own work as seen in terms of these categories and whether it was fairly characterised by means of them. They considered the categories reasonable and fair, if overlapping, and the spirit as well as the detail of their discussions and comments certainly provided a consensual basis for what follows. But it is, of course, for the reader to consider whether she/he will subscribe to this consensus.

I thus present in all the following sections of this chapter some theoretical perspectives, practical examples and critical insights that have resulted from these processes. In so doing I seek to use the categories not as ultimate classification but as a means to highlight significant issues and to point out strong relationships between and interesting gaps within the studies. Such presentation has as its *ultimate* end the clarifying of the nature of these tutors' practices, and of tutors' practices generally.

Theoretical perspectives

Because the selection of theoretical perspectives used to illuminate the practice reported in the studies is itself subjective (though systematic), the basis of this selection is here explained so that readers may consider my presentations in the light of it.

Remarkably, education tutors working in ITE do not, as a professional group, have clearly established, generally agreed, specific traditions of practice of their own, except of the most general practical kind, related to working in school. Arguably it is fitting that they borrow eclectically from theory and practice of teaching more generally and that they are constantly constructing both practice and theory in their own work. But since their expertise is clearly different in some respects from that of teachers, it is at least surprising that they have not attended more systematically to the principled bases of their work. Now that it is under threat, they may wish to do so — indeed, it seems vital that they do so.

In order to provide a basis for understanding and illuminating the work described in the studies presented here, I turned to the approaches, procedures and theoretical perspectives of Curriculum Studies. Here I selected from amongst a range of literature, using particularly the work of Reid (1979), and the more recent work of David Carr, and Wilfred Carr, and of Grundy (1987) which provides a most useful theoretical foundation for the work of curriculum deliberation and practice. I have also used in Chapter 9 perspectives from language study, writing on critical and creative thinking, and from professional development. As they meet these theoretical perspectives, readers will wish to weigh for themselves their significance and usefulness for my purpose.

(ii)

Tutors' intentions and their assumptions[1]

This section attempts to scrutinise tutors' views about their goals (longer-term aims) and intentions (more immediate concerns) in ITE. It considers particularly their espoused theories, and their theories-in-use about their roles, and confronts these with a range of perspectives on what student teachers should learn. (The word 'intentions' here signals a clear rejection of the notion that the end product of teaching can be entirely pre-specified in objectives.)

---

1. In all of the following, references to writers refer to their particular chapters, but references citing Robert Catt first refer to Chapter 4, while those citing Tom Sweeney first refer to Chapter 7.

Goals

We have seen from *Circulars 9/92* and *14/93* and the Education Act 1994 with its promotion of school-centred ITT, the government's view that the goals for ITE are to produce efficient deliverers of the National Curriculum in the classroom (See Chapter 1 above; Edwards 1992; and Fish 1995.) Against this backdrop probably all HE staff, and no doubt many teachers who are involved with ITE, irrespective of their specific views about how to achieve this, would argue for the same ends – that future teachers should understand those deep educational issues which ought to inform their practice rather than being drilled in skills and competences which they then have no knowledge of when and how to use. As Schnur and Golby say, they need to understand teaching:

> as an activity of social and moral significance, encapsulating 'know how' by placing it in its cultural context. Thus teachers need to know, and are entitled to know, how their work affects pupils, families and communities, how it concerns social justice, how it contributes, in short to the good life.
> (Schnur and Golby 1995, in press)

Probably, with Edwards (1992), Kelly (1993), D. Carr (1993) and Schnur and Golby (1995), most teacher educators would argue for the preparation of a professional by means of improving students' capacity for professional judgement and decision making rather than by providing extensive practice of skills in a single classroom – or even several. With them they would probably call for the exercise of insight, strategic understanding and critical thinking rather than effective performance of learnt skills. With them they would probably seek to develop practical wisdom rather than endlessly refined but situation-specific instrumental knowledge. In short, they would see the aims of ITE as changing the awareness and understanding of students in respect of themselves, of the nature of teaching and learning and of their practice.

  These, of course, are long-term aims. Learning to teach is an enterprise in which, in addition to practical experience, students need to stand back from practice and enter into on-going informed deliberation and reflection. It is here, I would argue, that the HE tutors' work is currently central and that the role of the university is vital in offering the arena for this operation and the resources and expertise in teaching and research to enrich this process. The basis of this work is the view that development of professional practice is achieved by knowing about in depth and understanding key professional issues, together with engaging in on-going conversation related to a variety of practical activities. David Carr expresses this most succinctly:

> even the most basic and routine of classroom tasks and skills cannot be happily disengaged from wider considerations of a philosophical, moral or evaluative kind about the precise nature of the benefit which we are trying to provide for children through education and about our larger purposes as educationalists with respect to that benefit.
> (Carr D. 1992, p.20)

He later adds:

> no teacher is likely to be a successful educator unless he has been to some extent sensitized to the larger ethical implications of the curricular package he has been charged to deliver through rational and informed reflection on his *role* and purpose as a teacher.
> (Carr D. 1992, p.21)

And later again he says that skills:

> acquire their real significance as enmeshed in a wider context of aims and objectives which are defined by reference to a complex network of public, social and moral duties and obligations which the teacher owes to children, parents, employing authorities and society at large.
> (Carr D. 1992, p.22)

When questions about the ends of teacher education are asked in relation to the case studies in Part 2 above, a sharp awareness of these issues is to be found. Hilma Rask, for example, talks of 'professional growth'; quotes Yeoman's comments about preparing students for a delicate relationship with other adults in the classroom and discusses the developing of student teachers' understanding of the nature of collaborative teamwork in the nursery. Robert Catt talks of 'structural principles', of 'the interrogation of and reflection' upon experience, and, the need to develop in students 'their practical knowledge, that is thinking on their feet, together with more deliberative reflection'. To do this, he says, 'they need to give due regard to historical, social and institutional contexts'. Christine Edwards seeks to develop in students an understanding of the levels and standards of work to be expected in children in music for Key Stages 1 and 2, to 'evaluate the appropriateness of activities' she offers and 'to decide for themselves' whether and how they might use them. Lynne Thorogood seeks to facilitate an understanding about the messages transmitted by displays of work beneath which lie important social and moral issues. Tom Sweeney seeks to provide a basis from which his students are confident in teaching drama. He explicitly wishes to 'establish firmly the principle of experiential learning so that students are in a position to gain insights into pupil achievement in drama and their own personal and professional development'. He also explicitly 'eschews a simple apprenticeship style of training in favour of an approach which aims to encourage students to generate their own future content and range of teaching styles'. In the workshop tutors suggested that it was important to enable students to 'come to know themselves in a professional role'.

If these are the overall goals, what were the individual intentions associated with tutors' specific practices?

Intentions

Specifically the studies show that tutors were seeking very different things from the government's narrow concern to offer skills training. But there is no consensus on such matters. Other colleagues have argued for the application of formal theory to practice (see, for example, Stones (1981 and 1992) who recommends the application of protocols gained from psychology to classroom situations). In the studies above tutors seek to develop students' ability to engage in practical discourse. They were seeking to involve students in ongoing conversations. Their intentions were to:

● help students to find their voices

● enable students to construct their own theories

● help them to transcend the specifics of one classroom

● enable students to travel confidently between theory and practice

● encourage them to handle thought and action, the specific and the general

● help them disentangle the normative (what ought to be) and the operative (what is)

160

● help students to harness critical thinking.

Illustrations of these intentions abound in the studies and are discussed in detail in Chapter 9 below. Hilma Rask argues that 'above all there must be critical discussion arising out of practice ... Such critical talk aims to make explicit connections between theory and practice in action'. Citing music as a subject with particular pressures in primary ITE, Christine Edwards argues that students often have very patchy knowledge themselves, cannot read up to compensate for this and need observation and involvement with children in schools, but not without detailed analysis and reflection. Tom Sweeney talks about providing for students 'opportunities for the development of a voice in discussion', and about encouraging them 'to generate questions, to problematise the situation and to develop further possibilities'. He notes that the ability to see practice as problematic is a distinguishing mark of a reflective practitioner. And Robert Catt states roundly that he and Tom are seeking to develop 'socially constructed and conversationally shared awareness and understanding'. He added, in the workshop, that he was concerned to achieve a developing understanding in students 'of the constructed nature of classroom activity and a concomitant awareness that practice can be changed'. There is much in the studies about conversation and much in the literature too. We shall look at this in detail in the next chapter. Meanwhile we should note that there is considered support from the literature of Curriculum Studies for this approach to practice. For example, Reid argues that it is important to see 'curriculum problems as uncertain practical problems that have to be treated by the exercise of practical reasoning' (Reid 1979, p.67). He also argues that these processes are educational and improve problem appreciation and calls for the introduction of key words like 'action', 'judgement', 'deliberation', 'appreciation', 'criticism', 'responsibility', 'argument' and 'justification' (Reid 1979, p.69). Such vocabulary clearly characterises the tutors' studies.

Values and beliefs

All the above aims and intentions, then, indicate the value-base of the writers of the studies. They are either expressed directly in the studies or the whole tenor of the presentation and the descriptions of their procedures in working with students provide evidence of this. Some more overtly recognise their reflective practitioner basis, others operate within it rather more intuitively. Some have a Curriculum Studies expertise, some do not. In this they are representative of education tutors in that they have a range of interests and expertise across age range, subject interests and views about and understanding of a tutor's work and of reflective practice generally. All, however, are alert to the social and moral issues embedded in the simplest of classroom actions and, in the very way they describe these, indicate their concerns. For example, Lynne is concerned that publicising the desired model of children's work by means of wall display amounts to taking control of what children will value and that teachers are often far less aware than children of 'messages embedded in displays'.

To look in more detail at their ways of working is to come closer to these values.

(iii)

The tutors' knowledge and personal qualities

It is difficult to make absolute distinctions between this and the following category, but it seems important to try to acknowledge in this interpretative survey the dimension of the tutors' own personal attributes (as evidenced in the studies) because they make an important contribution to the personal and professional development of student teachers. Tutors all clearly draw explicitly upon their own capacities, abilities, understandings and knowledge in working with students. This comes clearly through their writing and to some extent begins to suggest some key differences between what tutors can provide for students and what teachers in schools can offer them, thus highlighting the importance of students benefiting from both.

Perhaps most vital, because it is drawn upon in their overarching strategy, is the tutors' ability to travel between theory and practice, the general and the specific. This entails a *working knowledge* of significant theories about practice, about learning practice and about grounded theory. It also involves being comfortable about working at the level of principle and in helping students to reach that level. And it involves the ability to present practical issues in problematic terms in order to engage students in deeper levels of discussion. This in turn rests on wide knowledge and understanding of practice in a range of differing settings. As Lynne says, for example, this enables her to 'see beyond the here and now' to recognise the significance of teachers' practical decisions about display in terms of social justice and motivation and to be alert to their influence on children's minds and imaginations. It also demands knowledge of the procedures of practical educational discourse. And it draws on expertise in analysis and critical thinking. It depends upon experience of uncovering what lies under the surface of students' 'superficially pedestrian' discussions. Tutors have the experience to spot potential in students' comments, and the skills of enabling them to learn through practice. Tutors have the opportunity to work with a wide range of schools and classes and are able to harness the results of this to enrich their work. Hilma, for example, talks of the 'essence' of practical settings; Lynne is concerned about the influence of display on the wider school community, parents and governors. Many also work with practising teachers on professional development enterprises in in-service courses. The interplay between ITE and INSET has always provided much food for thought and useful examples of practice for work in ITE, as we see specifically in Lynne's study.

In addition to this there is the important specialist knowledge that tutors bring to their work with students. This knowledge relates to wide settings and usually includes specialist subject knowledge and specialist pedagogic knowledge. Here, it is important to note that, confounding popular scepticism, the work of these tutors shows that scholarly activity, far from being incompatible with successful practice, can be *about* practice, to the benefit of both. Most tutors work in schools in a research capacity and not only bring the processes and the results of this to their work with students but also engage in more public debate and contribute to both professional and academic literature. Christine notes that 'the broadening perspectives, curriculum initiatives, research into ways of understanding and assessing children's musical learning, have been led by college and university departments'. Such writing often begins with a practical problem at the tutor's level. Robert has knowledge of and contributes to writings about conversation analysis, and said in the workshop that he is 'currently entangled in considering the kinds of power relations that inhabit discourse in seminars' and is 'trying to provide more space for talk in a variety of discourse styles' in lectures. Tom is 'seeking ways of supporting students' development of the capacity to reflect systematically, which involves careful preparation and sensitivity on the part of the tutor'. Tom and Robert together contribute to professional journals. Lynne writes about language and linguistics.

In Schnur and Golby's terms, these tutors are consumers as well as producers of research (Schnur and Golby 1995, in press). They are all familiar with writing and thinking which is at the cutting edge of developing understandings about the nature of learning to teach – particularly in their own subject areas. Tom and Robert base their work explicitly on that of Schön (1987), and his ideas about reflective practice. Hilma refers to recent literature, research and her own investigations across schools. Christine refers to a range of important recent research on music education and the arts more generally. She too has a range of contacts to draw upon as a result of her previous INSET role. She has a rich knowledge of specialist skills and techniques. Her work with students is 'informed and supported by the methodology and curriculum materials' which she helped to develop under ILEA. Tom is deeply interested in the nature of arts in education and draws on his knowledge of the recent surveys and research conducted in relation to this theme.

Of considerable importance too is tutors' knowledge of how HE operates; of course design for professional education; and of how students behave – including an understanding of the tensions, feelings and problems endemic in the struggle to voice, explore and reconstruct values and attitudes. Tom and Robert refer to their understanding of the nature and philosophy of the course the students are on. Robert expresses little surprise at some of the issues which emerge as important for the students.

In short, tutors relate their practical work in school and with students to work in college and to the wider teaching and research community. All work regularly in schools – not for the vacant reason of fulfilling government requirements, but for proper reasons related to refining their understanding of and ideas about practice, and thus improving their contributions to teacher development and research. All have proved themselves in advanced academic work. And this is only part of their academic responsibilities. They also teach across a range of in-service programmes, visit other ITE courses elsewhere in the country (often in the role of external examiners) and work with teachers or teacher educators in other countries.

If these are some of the bases upon which tutors work with students, what then can be said in an overview of their activities?

(iv)

The tutors' activities

The writers of the case studies provide evidence of their activities in working as tutors in five key aspects of practice. **Firstly,** they select, and provide the purposeful activities that enable students to experience and focus on chosen aspects of practice. (Contrary to the popular image, for example, we see Tom and Robert ensuring that their project was rooted in practice by operating it first with pupils in school.) They then used a wider repertoire of activities with the students than with the pupils 'in order to demonstrate the range of choices available to teachers who may need to work with a variety of classes in a variety of settings', and thus attend 'to the professional concerns of students who want to experiment with various teaching strategies for different groups of children'. Christine took the class while students observed. Hilma tells us about role-play exercises where she seeks to 'outline possible scenarios in early years classroom contexts and invite group and individual exploration of possible actions and the consequences of such actions'. She points out that sessions such as this 'aim to provide a safe place in which to take risks, and to explore, in a more considered way, approaches to dealing with adults in a team setting'. She gives as examples, dealing with confrontation, negotiating change, managing difficult or distressed parents or working with an entrenched colleague. In none of this is practice engaged in for its own sake, however. Indeed, tutors' main interest is clearly in systematically fostering specific aspects of learning through experience, which they share with students. Their **second** key activity then is engaging students in practical discourse. (The detail of this is provided in Chapter 9.)

Thirdly, they engage students in carefully focussed writing and reading about the practical. In this, as in the practice and the discussion of it, they offer students a sound model, by being visibly involved in both activities themselves. There is currently much work by tutors in this field and much of it demonstrates very clearly how carefully focussed, practically centred, reflective and deliberative writing can provide an important means of learning for students and can bring them to recognise their own views, beliefs and theories (see, for example, Boud, Keogh and Walker 1985; Carter 1994; Tripp 1993). An example of the importance of student writing is highlighted in Chapter 9 below.

Fourthly, and again offering a good model, they engage in critical thinking and self-criticism, providing examples of opening their professional judgements up to critique even as they work with the group. For example, Christine Edwards makes the point that 'while encouraging them to reflect on their teaching and become more self-critical, I also had to adjust to my new role and rethink the way I work'.

She demonstrates this later by saying how she will improve future visits. She also shows how she takes risks — as she would wish students also to do — in her work with the class of children. Robert Catt and Tom Sweeney clearly use critical incidents and report on the 'glows' and 'wobbles' of these in their own work, offering open self-criticism. (What is not clear here, however, is the extent to which they draw to their students' attention both their reflection-in-action as they work with students or their written and published work (and experiences of its processes) as they tutor students about their written work.)

Fifthly, tutors engage in investigations of their practice — of which, of course, the chapters in Part 2 are examples. It is interesting to note, too, that in the case of Robert and Tom, they actually involve students in video-ing their work and share the critical viewing of the results, the students knowing that the 'evaluations' are partly for their own work and partly for the tutors'. Predictably, this is highly motivating for students. (It is interesting to speculate about how much more valuable work would come from engaging students and tutors in joint research.)

Good practice, however, also includes knowing when to withdraw. The last word here should go to Hilma, who in the workshop, said: 'I often think that the best learning has taken place when the tutor has stepped back.'

(v)

Aspects of tutors' practices: a critical overview

The following offers a brief critique of the studies, and focusses specifically on aspects that may be more broadly typical of tutors' practices in HE. It will be for the reader (and the partners in ITE) to consider how far these studies are indeed representative.

Some clear characteristics

Some very clear statements can be made about these studies, but they inevitably raise in their wake some contestable issues, and these are considered in the following subsection. One important general characteristic which should be noted first is that these tutors do not operate as has been portrayed in the media caricatures of their work. For example, they do not:

- tell students how to teach
- offer them training in skills
- work at the level of description only
- offer them prescriptions
- offer them certainties
- offer simple explanations about, or increasingly sophisticated skills of, 'delivery'
- offer them theory and abstract truth-seeking
- teach them political ideology
- offer formal theory to be applied in the classroom.

Indeed, instead of all this, all tutors clearly worked in partnership *with* students rather than *on* students as they sought to enable them to explore choices, to analyse and to think about practice. In fact, a deep thoughtfulness about teaching and learning comes strongly through the studies. There is a clear concern to focus on the practical, in that they all start from action and experience, but from there they quickly raise theoretical issues about teaching and learning which lie beneath. Tutors are sharply aware of the need to reach beyond the technical aspects of practice, and in this they are helped by being able to travel comfortably between theory and practice, the specific and the general and ITE and INSET activities and in knowing how HE operates as a system. Clearly, too, tutors' knowledge-base and expertise, their research activities and their theoretical and research knowledge are important resources for students, as is the fact that they are able to work with students at a distance from the school classroom and enable students to take time to explore ideas.

It is important to note here that although they have a working knowledge of educational theories and their relationship to practice, the expertise they draw upon is based perhaps more in subject areas than in Curriculum Studies itself.

The overall success of tutors in developing students' understanding is also amply evidenced. In this they call upon the five activities mentioned above (the selection of specific practice experiences for students; the engagement of students in practical discourse; the involvement of students in carefully focussed writing; the offering of a good model in respect of self-criticism; and the involvement of both parties in the investigation of professional practice). In all of this, students' and tutors' achievements are seen as bound up together, and many of the tutors' achievements in respect of students' learning are seen in terms of enabling students to find their own voices. Currently, this is a particularly fashionable focus in ITE (see Carter 1994; Hoover 1994; and Johnston 1994). In the workshop Hilma said that she felt something had been achieved when a student voiced a dilemma, a problem or started to talk in a self-questioning way. And there are examples in the studies of students showing awareness of what they are learning and how.

Further, tutors' achievements are not only about students' learning (which is charted in detail in the following chapter). It should also be noted that they speak too of their own achievements and their own learning as a result of working with students. For example, Hilma, acknowledging that it had been a privilege to see students' growth and learning, added: 'The interviews proved to be most enriching for me professionally ... This opened up areas for further reflection on my own part, about the nature of ITE and the particular needs of early years students'. In the workshop all tutors declared that they had gained from writing the case studies. They characterised this as struggling to find their own voices and to make sense of their own practice and research. But, of course, it would be mere 'contemplation' (see Fish 1995, p.173), to seek to do so without seeking also to relate their work to a broader view of the tutors' role in ITE. How, then, can we make sense of these *aspects* of tutors' practice?

A vital problem

The studies have highlighted some important aspects of education tutors' roles, and this in itself is a major contribution to current debates − and there is more that is to be said in the following chapter about the tutors' key activities in practical discourse. But they have also shown us a problem. It is as if in their successful work they have each built a boat − each of which clearly rides the water well. But beneath their individual constructions flows a river dangerous to craft that navigate alone and lack a landing place. They need to be more than linked together in a flotilla − they need lines to the Curriculum Studies shore, and to that of philosophers through whom they can get to know the country through which they sail. And, in this, these studies are particular examples of the general case. Lack of proper attachment to the shore is not *these* tutors' problem, but the problem of the role of tutors generally in ITE. Although there is tacit knowledge about the education tutor's role in ITE, there is no rationale for it which is public and explicit. And there is no overall framework either within which to make sense of their practice. The practice of teaching has long been generally understood to consist of certain commonly performed activities (even though there might be dispute about the balance and emphasis amongst them). But what of the practice of tutoring? These tutors' studies provide us with some particulars – *they* could do no more. But they also highlight the vital need for much more work in this area.

This problem is evidenced, for example, in an absence of common vocabulary and ideas through which students' thinking about complex matters might be extended. There is, too, an ambivalence about how extensive and of what character ought to be the critical dimension of work with student teachers.

For example the term 'critical' and – more particularly – 'critique' has a strongly ideological association, yet the activities of criticism should surely be open to use by all.

Professional judgement provides a striking illustration here. It particularly emerges from the studies as a central matter. Not only are tutors seeking to develop it in their students, but they are concomitantly seeking to exercise, draw attention to, and develop their own. But there is no evidence, amongst the studies in the language used to describe these matters (either in their writing or in their discussions with students), of *shared* vocabulary and theoretical perspectives from (for example) Curriculum Studies and philosophy that would take students' thinking further and enable them to consider such useful distinctions as those between strategic judgements and practical judgements.

Neither is it clear how far tutors actually take students into the moral, social and political realms, or how far they should take them. There is talk in the studies about the importance of these matters, but little real evidence of the content of such discussions with students, and no discussion of any framework that might help tutors decide how far to go in this. But embracing uncertainty is not about shutting out knowledge, but about recognising the ambiguities in that which is known. It would seem that tutors need overall broadly shared frameworks to help them see where their particular contribution – and that of the teacher – might lie.

Clearly, there is a concern for and detailed information about how tutors engage students in practical discourse (see Chapter 9 below). But, again, it is not clear how aware they all are of the *principles* upon which they work. Indeed, I conclude as a result of the shared workshop that some of this work may be at an intuitive level. Again, there seems to be an urgent need for further investigations of these matters.

A need for studies which focus on the more difficult matters of ITE, of students failing to grasp issues, inability to engage in self-criticism and refusal to come to terms with self-knowledge, also surfaces as a result of tutors' work – although Robert and Tom certainly show something of these problems. Again there is much that could be investigated in this whole area.

Meanwhile, the following is an attempt to offer at least some perspectives that might be of use in understanding and exploring these matters.

Some useful theoretical perspectives

The following philosophical ideas offer some enlightenment about professional judgement and some very useful distinctions that might serve to provide the beginnings of a rationale for the work of the tutor – which must surely begin with some broad view of the nature of the practices in which the tutors are engaged, and which must surely proceed to distinguish these from the work of teachers.

For example, the work of David Carr (1993) and Grundy (1987) both offer useful clarification. The virtue of practical wisdom (or, in Aristotle's terms, *phronesis*) is a major issue, for example, in considering professional judgement and how to develop it. Carr refers to *phronesis* as 'a kind of active *practical* enquiry ... concerned with determining what should be *done* for the best' in a practical situation, as opposed to theoretical enquiry which is 'concerned with establishing truths about the world or explaining the order of things in some *disengaged speculative way'* [italics mine] (see Carr, D. 1993, p.264). He reminds us that:

> for Aristotle, the goal of theoretical enquiry is distinguished by its concern for the discovery of *truth,* whereas that of practical enquiry is marked by its concern to determine and bring about the *good.*
> (Carr, D. 1993, p.263)

He adds that in order to achieve overall practical competence (as opposed to individual competences) professionals need to be initiated into 'neither a form of *theoretical science* (though aspects of such sciences may inform [them]) nor a kind of *practical science* (though technological and other considerations ... are also proper educational goals), but a form of *moral enquiry* (see Carr, D. 1993, pp.264–5). Wilfred Carr argues that 'deliberating well is a mark of *phronesis*' (Carr W. 1987, p.172). And so critical and creative thinking, and procedures for systematic reflection, also need to be learnt by intending teachers. They are highlighted in tutors' studies, but there is a sense that something further is needed to provide a coherent rationale for this work.

The work of Grundy (1987) offers a useful framework for making meaning out of curriculum practice. Drawing on ideas of Habermas, Grundy offers a clear idea of three systems of knowledge generation and organisation, which could give some shape to the ITE curriculum and enable tutors to see where their contribution lies in it, and to distinguish that from the work of teachers. The three systems are: the technical, the practical and the emancipatory. Only a brief idea of them can be given here.

Grundy shows how Habermas's 'technical approach' is concerned with questions about what the practical worker should do on the spot. Its seeks to improve outcomes by improving skills. This approach allows knowledge to be controlled by one group within education and sees success in terms of effectiveness and efficiency. Here theory directs, confirms and legitimates practice. Here the only judgement that can be operated by the practitioner is strategic judgement – about what to do to attain a given end. This is what we have earlier called the technical-rational approach. Those who follow it practise according to rules and use their skills to a pre-determined end. Any curriculum for a practitioner under this approach is best designed on the basis of Stenhouse's product model (see Stenhouse 1975). The training for a practitioner of this kind would be skills or competences training. And those already operating such skills could easily initiate others into them without outside help.

By contrast, Grundy suggests that, via Habermas's 'practical approach', we can see practice as guided by choice which in turn is guided by a disposition towards what is 'good'. This involves an aspect of moral consciousness. There is greater choice here for the practitioner. The practitioner here would break rules if she/he judged it necessary for 'good'. Here the practical decisions have to be made in the actual situation. This involves what he calls 'practical judgement' which is exercised through deliberation (or reflection). According to Grundy (1993, p.65), 'Deliberation incorporates processes of interpretation and making meaning of a situation so that appropriate action can be decided upon and taken.'

All participants have equal rights in interpreting or making meaning
out of a situation. The practitioner chooses action guided by personal
judgement, having understood the situation. This means that practitioners are educated in ways described in the tutors' studies above.
Theory provides a guide not a direction, and curriculum planning
is on the basis of Stenhouse's process model (see Stenhouse 1975).
Judgement, though not a skill, can be developed through processes of reflection. Meaning-making in a democratic environment
is vital – and is helped by writing as well as talking. Further,
Grundy shows that, as well as practical knowledge arising directly
through reflection upon practice, Habermas's 'practical interest'
encourages the development of knowledge through the bringing to
consciousness of implicit theory, thus providing a more consciously
rational basis for action (Grundy 1987, p.77). Much of this is familiar
and could provide a detailed rationale for tutors' practices in ITE as
described in the above studies.

The third or 'emancipatory' orientation towards the curriculum
serves to raise some difficult questions about tutors' practices, about
which tutors probably need to reflect generally. This approach
engages students in the active creation of knowledge along with the
teacher. Here teaching and learning are regarded as problematic,
the teacher is taught in a dialogue along with the student, and
both theory and practice must both be open to critical scrutiny.
Here dialogue is a vital means of learning, and a curriculum is
not a written plan but an active process in which planning, acting
and evaluating are reciprocally related. Here, significantly, the
word 'critique' is taken to mean a more fundamental questioning
of both theory and practice than is implied in the 'practical approach'
and in the more traditional usage of the term 'critical thinking'.
By this means, Grundy and her fellow thinkers distinguish sharply
between broadly 'reproductive' and radically 'transformative'
approaches to education. But in fact in the studies the tutors utilise
strategies from this approach without necessarily subscribing to
the entire philosophy. (And this is not unreasonable, since if
all theory and practice are to be considered critically and used eclectically, then so is the 'emancipatory approach'.) What Grundy
offers us, however, is a means of understanding where these ideas
come from. Though that is not to deny that some tutors clearly
already do.

Grundy argues that the 'emancipatory approach' provides for
authentic learning by students as opposed to the 'coopted agreement'
which characterises other approaches (Grundy 1987, p.125). Here
knowledge is socially constructed, the teacher recognises 'moral

172

constraint in the extent to which student learning may be coerced'
(Grundy 1987, p.127), and the learner can thus control the learning
situation. The locus of control for making judgements about the
quality and meaningfulness of the work lie with the participants in
the learning situation, and there is freedom to question accepted
wisdom, recognise that things are not as they seem to be and
develop a sophisticated critical consciousness where questioning
leads to investigation which leads to critical insight. This authentic
critique 'looks back at theory and, while trying to make meaning
of it, critically examines its value for practice' (Grundy 1987,
p.132). Here theory is looked to for information but not for
direction. This approach 'brings enlightenment concerning the real
conditions of existence' (Grundy 1987, p.157), and transforms
consciousness – enables us to see the constraints within which our
practice occurs and to break out of habitual ways of seeing things
and of acting.

Thus Habermas's ideas – as conveyed by Grundy, certainly help
us to make sense of some of the activities reported by tutors in their
studies. Exactly how far this approach is of use in ITE is a matter
for debate, but it is important that tutors should engage in some
investigation of their work and open it to public debate.

It is clear, then, that in sharing their studies publicly, the tutors
have already provided an important service for readers as well as
themselves by alerting us to important aspects of their work and to
areas which need further development. Armed with this overview,
and as a small contribution to the wider enterprise of teacher preparation, we can now turn to the details of a central part of tutors'
work which may have a major significance for ITE however it is
constituted in future.

References

Atkinson, P. and Delamont, S. (1986) 'Bread and dreams or bread and
circuses? A critique of case study research in education', in Hammersley,
M. (Ed.) (1986) *Controversies in classroom research*. Milton Keynes:
Open University Press, pp.238–55.
Boud, D., Keogh, R. and Walker, D. (1985) *Reflection turning experience
into learning*. London: Kogan Page.
Carr, D. (1992) 'Four dimensions of educational professionalism',
Westminster Studies in Education, 15 (10), pp.19–33.
Carr, D. (1993) 'Questions of competence', *British Journal of Educational
Studies,* 41 (3), pp.253–71.
Carr, W. (1987) 'What is an educational practice?', *Journal of Philosophy
of Education,* 21 (2), pp.163–75.

Carter, K. (1994) 'Preservice teachers' well-remembered events and the acquisition of event-structured knowledge', *Journal of Curriculum Studies,* **26** (3), pp.235–52.

Edwards, T. (1992) *Change and reform in initial teacher education.* (Briefing Paper No. 9) London: National Commission on Education.

Fish, D. (1995) *Quality mentoring for student teachers: a principled approach to practice.* London: David Fulton.

Gilroy, P. (1993) 'Reflections on Schön: an epistemological critique and a practical alternative', in Gilroy, P. and Smith, M. (Eds) (1993) *International Analysis of Teacher Education: Journal of Education for Teaching,* **19** (4/5), pp.83–9.

Grundy, S. (1987) *Curriculum: product or praxis.* London: Falmer Press.

Hoover, L.A. (1994) 'Reflective writing as a window on preservice teachers' thought processes', *Teaching and Teacher Education,* **10** (1), pp.83–93.

Johnston, S. (1994) 'Conversations with student teachers – enhancing the dialogue of learning to teach', *Teaching and Teacher Education,* **10** (1), pp.71–82.

Kelly, A.V. (1993) 'Education as a field of study in a university: challenge, critique, dialogue, debate', *Journal of Education for Teaching,* **19** (2), pp.125–39.

Reid, W. (1979) *Thinking about the curriculum: the nature and treatment of curriculum problems.* London: Routledge and Kegan Paul.

Schnur, J. and Golby, M. (1995, in press) 'Teacher education: a university mission?' *Journal of Teacher Education,* **46** (1).

Schön, D. (1987) *Educating the reflective practitioner.* London: Jossey Bass.

Stenhouse, L. (1975) *An introduction to curriculum research and development.* London: Heineman.

Stenhouse, L. (1980) 'The study of samples and the study of cases', *British Educational Research Journal,* **4** (1), pp.1–16.

Stenhouse, L. (1982) 'The conduct, analysis and reporting of case study in educational research and evaluation', in McCormick, R. (Ed.) (1982) *Calling education to account.* London: Heinemann, pp.261–73.

Stenhouse, L. (1985) 'A note on case study and educational practice', in Burgess R. (Ed.) (1985) *Field methods in the study of education.* Lewes: Falmer, pp.211–33.

Stones, E. (1981) *Psychopedagogy.* London: Methuen.

Stones, E. (1992) *Quality teaching: a sample of cases.* London: Routledge.

Tickle, L. (1993) 'Capital T teaching', in Elliott, J. (Ed.) (1993) *Reconstructing teacher education: teacher development.* London: Falmer Press, pp.110–24.

Tripp, D. (1993) *Critical incidents in teaching: developing professional judgement.* London: Routledge.

CHAPTER 9

Engaging Students in Practical Discourse: the Enterprise and its Demands

Introduction

The education tutor's role is, in general, diverse and endless, but many see the development of practical discourse as a central activity, and this is certainly suggested by Grundy (1987). Such development is vital in the preparation of a professional with knowledge of profession-wide issues, who can discuss them in a range of professional contexts (with colleagues, parents and school governors) and who can weigh up the possibilities for practical action and understand the various values that underlie it. The central role of practical discourse in ITE is also a major reason why working from distance-learning packs seems a strange way of preparing to become a teacher.

Wade, at the start of an article reporting research on what motivates student teachers to participate in seminars, reports that in developing reflection, 'class discussion is probably the most prevalent and potentially useful approach'. By class discussion she does mean practical discourse, because she adds: 'the dialectical nature of discussion makes it distinctly suited to two key components of reflection, viewing a situation from multiple perspectives and seeing alternatives to one's thinking' (see Wade 1994, p.231). In a very useful literature survey on discussion she says:

> The literature on critical reflection thus far has treated classroom discussion a bit like an old dog sleeping on the back porch. Predictably, it is there, has always been there, a comforting presence one can

count on that is rarely given more than a pat on the head. In two reviews of various means for promoting critical reflection, discussion as a strategy is never specifically mentioned, (Adler, 1991; Zeichner, 1987).
(Wade 1994, p.232)

She adds later that 'little information about the effective use of this strategy has been detailed'. It is necessary, however, to be rather more specific about this. There certainly seems to be little work as yet in detail on the use of group discussion to promote reflection and deliberation − that is, to engage in practical discourse, but there has been over the years a long tradition of study of the group and the seminar in HE. Significant examples include: Abercrombie and Terry (1978); Bligh (1986); Nias (1987); and Rudduck (1978). However, the work of Abercrombie and Terry focusses mainly on the behaviour of small groups (the nurture of group discussion, supportive nature of the group, empathy, self-awareness, control of content and participation, authority and dependency), while the work of Rudduck looks at participation, monitoring, leaderless groups and training students for group work. She does look more closely at the content of discussion, but the subjects under discussion in her groups did not include teachers' practical work. The work of Nias, however, does focus on professional improvement through reflection and the support of a group (although in INSET not ITE) and, in this, she draws on the work of Foulkes and of Habermas in talking about how: 'roped together by a common commitment to the exploration and understanding of their own experience, members of a group can support one another across the chasm of personal redefinition and modification', and how 'sharing, communication and growth are inextricably linked' (Nias 1987, p.2). But Nias does not set out to investigate the details of how this happens within group work. Wade's conclusion, then, that 'further explanation of the use of discussion is warranted' and 'discussion as a strategy for enhancing critical enquiry deserves greater attention' (Wade 1994, p.232) does seem right. She is no doubt also right in calling for 'case studies which focus on individual students' participation patterns and analyses of student thinking in response to different types of discussion methods' and for 'studies which explore techniques to identify effective questions, statements or topic foci for fostering critical reflection' (Wade 1994, p.241).

It is possible that the work of Osterman and Kottkamp (1993) on nurturing reflection might also be usefully employed in such studies, as might Habermas's contribution in the shape of his idea of the

Ideal Speech Situation. Arguing that the meaning-making and interpretation that are central to understanding are fostered by *critical*
discussion, Grundy describes the Ideal Speech Situation for this as
one 'in which all participants have equal opportunities to engage in
dialogue', where this freedom is established through 'concern for
the distribution of power within the groups and the opportunity
afforded to any member of the group to challenge any aspect of the
discussion', and where talk is not merely descriptive and reflective
but also critical in the emancipatory sense (Grundy 1987, p.117).
Just how far practical discourse in ITE needs to be emancipatory
is, of course, a value-based matter for critical debate. What is clear
is that discussion about it has not taken place on any scale.

This chapter then, making a small contribution in this area, looks
in detail at the educational aspects of practical discourse as revealed
in the studies, at how tutors engaged students in it, and what they
achieved as a result. It focusses centrally on practical discourse in
group settings.

(i)

Clarifying the nature of practical discourse

This section will attempt to clarify what is meant by practical discourse, and will look at some key activities and useful questions
associated with it.

Some definitions

By practical discourse is meant discussion of and reasoning about the
practical. This is not a matter of manipulating logic as, for example,
in challenging fallacies and unsupported assertion for the sake of
proving prowess in debate. It is rather about considering beliefs,
values, assumptions; about deciding between alternative interpretations; about weighing up current circumstances in order to take
new action; and about being able to justify actions in moral terms.
This process may be used within either the 'practical' or the 'emancipatory approach' described above. It often uses dialectics – the
bringing together of polar distinctions in order to stimulate clearer
thinking. It often aims at working to a resolution in which understanding of the reasons for opposing views (rather than reaching

simple consensus) is the only possible end. This may involve an oscillation between moral judgement and concrete action and lead to a modification of one and a clarification of the other. Such dialectic may emerge naturally as students come to recognise the great diversity of values and beliefs held amongst them. But it often has to be highlighted and focussed upon by a tutor because there is a tendency amongst students (and even some teachers) to expect to work towards consensus.

Practical discourse is achieved through dialogue, though not all dialogue in ITE is practical discourse. Dialogues between TP supervisor and student ought normally to come under the heading of practical discourse, but here the perspectives are limited to two or three participants. Much of this chapter is concerned with discussion in seminar groups.

Johnston quotes Gitlin (1990, pp.447–8) as providing some useful points to distinguish dialogue from talk or conversation. Gitlin, using the language of the emancipatory approach, apparently argues that a pre-condition for dialogue is that 'all participants see the discourse as important and have a say in determining its course'. Dialogue is also seen as the means whereby participants work together to understand the subject being discussed, rather than a situation where one actor is pitted against another. Finally Gitlin maintains that dialogue would 'make pre-judgements apparent' so that their critical testing can empower the participants to 'challenge taken-for-granted notions that influence the way they see the world and judge their practice' (see Johnston 1994, p.81).

Bridges et al. (1986) writing in the context of assessment and appraisal, and James (1989) writing in the context of student profiling, both raise interesting issues about distinctions between dialogue and negotiation, which are also pertinent here. Both activities are to do with face-to-face interaction. But there are important differences, and it is dialogue that better characterises practical discourse. Negotiation is essentially seen in both articles as a political activity on the part of the tutor 'about what we could agree to do or to allow', while 'dialogue was an epistemological activity concerned with truth and understanding' and whose objective was not agreement or consensus but a clear perception of the evidence or grounds for belief and a 'richer view of the valuation or interpretation which might be set on that evidence'. Such definitions perhaps will help us to be alert to what tutors are seeking to do, (see especially, James 1989, pp.157–8).

178

Some key activities

Reid, writing from within what Grundy, following Habermas, would
have distinguished as the 'practical approach', offers useful broad
perspectives on the processes involved in practical reasoning (deliberation) which is a central aspect of practical discourse. He argues
that curriculum problems (problems about designing, implementing
and evaluating curricula) are practical problems which are moral
rather than technical in nature (see Reid 1979, p.29). He suggests
that solutions to curriculum problems must be found in 'an inter-
active consideration of means and ends' (Reid 1979, p.42). He goes
on to show that most curriculum problems are 'uncertain practical
problems'. These are questions that have to be answered, but the
grounds on which decisions should be made are uncertain. In
answering them we have to take account of the existing state of
affairs, the situation-specific and unique character of them. Because
they are value-based, he argues, curriculum problems will 'compel us
to adjudicate between competing goals and values'. Further, we can
never predict the outcomes of the solution chosen, but the grounds
for our decision are not that the *activities* are but that the *goal* is
desirable. Practical reasoning, in Reid's terms is:

> an intricate and skilled intellectual and social process whereby, indi-
> vidually or collectively, we identify the questions to which we must
> respond, establish grounds for deciding on answers, and then choose
> among the available solutions.
> (Reid 1979, p.43)

It seems on the surface like an everyday activity, and we thus tend
to undervalue and make little effort to understand it.

As Wade reports, some writers have offered perspectives on
key components of the teacher's (tutor's) role including the establishment of 'an encouraging classroom climate, waiting for student
comments, and responding with empathetic, accepting, or clarifying
remarks' (see Costa 1990; and Wade 1994, p.232). In order to
promote 'a true discussion, characterized by openness, freedom,
equality, respect and truth', participants are encouraged in expressing
their opinion, to examine various viewpoints with intention to
further knowledge or judgement about the issue. (This verges more
on Habermas's 'emancipatory approach'.) Wade also makes the
point that:

it is important for teacher educators to encourage critique of ideas and opinions while at the same time honoring students' perspectives as legitimate and valuable [and that tutors should] require students to subject their ideas to analysis and evaluation by their peers.
(Wade 1994, p.240)

Johnston, discussing dialogue between supervisor and TP student, argues that:

dialogue must be collaborative, focusing on the student teacher's images of teaching and reconstructing those images as the problematic nature of teaching brings inconsistencies and contradictions to light. Student teaching should be a process of re-constructing visions of practice.
(Johnston 1994, p.81)

Reid (showing how the practical approach can regress to the technical) points out the strong temptation in discussion of practical issues to reduce uncertain curriculum problems to simple procedural problems and to find simple methodological solutions to them, or to ignore the complexity and declare an agreed goal or principle (like, for example, the current competences), and work towards consensus about it (see Reid 1979, pp.21−4). These moves cover over, but do not address, the uncertainty at the core of the practical. He indicates that getting students to move away from asking for simple practical answers and on to considering procedures and seeking principles is a mark of progress in practical discourse.

But getting students to ask questions at the level of principle assumes that tutors have a clear grasp of the different sorts of questions that are useful for this purpose. It is Carr who offers help here.

Some useful questions

David Carr (1993) offers four useful kinds of questions central to practical discourse:

Practical questions: questions about what to do or how to do it − for example 'What *do* I *do* now?' (This seeks direction on how to act at the moment.)

Procedural questions: questions seeking suggestions about

180

	methods – for example 'What *might* I do now?' (What are the procedural possibilities from amongst which I might choose?)
Prudential questions:	questions asking for adjudication between procedures and amongst the questioner's own preferences – for example 'What *should* I do now?' (What best suits me and my purpose? – even: 'What fain would I do now?')
Moral and ethical questions:	questions asking what is right and just to do – for example: 'What *ought* I to do now?' (What ought I to do for the sake of justice and goodness for and on behalf of other people?)

David Carr underlines the importance of his final category of question for teacher *education*. It would seem, in fact, that the last three of these four are essentially useful in the 'practical approach' to meaning-making, since, by contrast, the 'emancipatory approach' would take the view that these questions were themselves problematic. Reid's work supports David Carr, since Reid says that a teacher is 'a person engaged in an activity with moral ends' who must be able to justify his/her intentions and activities (Reid 1979, p.15). Carr makes the point that just as the failure of a teacher 'to respect children is not a failure of a skill or technique, but a failure of moral attitude or value, so it is not a failure of *skill* if a teacher cannot locate his teaching in a wider context of educational considerations, but a failure of *understanding*' (David Carr 1993, p.267). In fact, the only point at issue between these writers is the extent of the understanding to be fostered in ITE.

I suggest that the studies described in Part 2 above, and the illustration of its principled basis offered below, show something of the development of practical reasoning in students (mainly at the 'practical approach' level) and indicate that preparing students for these procedures constitutes a major contribution to ITE. I suggest too, at the more general level, that the evidence – so far at least – is that, while their work may need further development, tutors' expertise, knowledge-base and wide-ranging educational operations currently enable them (probably better than most teachers) to fulfil this role in ITE. This experience and expertise (together with acknowledgement of other relevant expertise) should influence future arrangements about the distribution of the ITE programme between partners.

(ii)

Developing practical discourse: tutors' practices

The sorts of strategies that bring students to confront procedural, prudential and moral questions then are those which call for the exploration of choices, which seek analysis and critical thinking (in the more traditional sense) and which enable students to develop socially constructed and conversationally shared awareness and understanding (which allows for but does not require thinking at an emancipatory level). The following paragraphs explore how tutors seek to achieve this.

An overarching strategy

The essential overarching strategy for the work involves managing a dialectic of the general and the particular so that students relate their practical classroom and school work to wider contexts. Hilma Rask notes that 'the taught course and the period of sustained school experience are both shown to play a vital role' in students' personal growth and that teaching practice files provide a rich resource and offer powerful first hand illustrations of their experience. She also makes the important point that 'students currently have opportunities to move between the experiences of being in the role of the teacher in the classroom and being a student in a college-based setting'. She adds: 'Stepping outside the immediate context of the classroom has an important role [in student teachers' learning]. At best in ITE there is a constant interplay between taught course and school experience through which students are encouraged to draw out personal theories from practice.' Robert Catt and Tom Sweeney aim 'to provide space and structured opportunities for observation, reflection and discussion so that [students] will begin to develop an informed understanding of the profession in which they are now involved'. (Note that they write about a profession-wide, not about a 'classroom-narrow', view.) Their Education Studies programme involves students in understanding the principles of good practice demonstrated through role-play and response to video-taped examples of teachers at work. Though we are not privy to the details, it is clear that Lynne's discussions with her TP student range between the classroom, school and wider issues about display. After Tom's role-playing of the late and disgruntled tutor, the 'subsequent relief allows a sound basis for shared discussion of productive organisational strategies'. Tom's and Robert's 'detectives'project acknowledges and values the work of schools and the importance of a 'dynamic and mutually supportive relationship between theory and practice in schools and colleges'.

Setting the context

It will be clear from this that certain general conditions are necessary to enable this key strategy of a dialectic of the particular and the general to be successful. For example, the context for this work must be distanced from the practical arena. Students need to be in a situation where listening and talking or writing freely are possible and are given due time and weight, and where there is proper space for reflection and for learning from it. They need to be able to take risks, either to discuss in a safe and democratic environment or know that their writing will be considered seriously and under neutral conditions (without being judged by those with partisan attitudes to particular schools, classrooms, pupils, colleagues and a particular teaching style).

Crucially, this means working in groups (what Nias (1987) calls social settings). She makes the point that we need other people's perspectives to make us aware of the egocentricity of our own. This therefore means establishing a group atmosphere which supports and extends learning (setting the tone of mutual trust, of humility in exploration, of democratic rights for all, of being open to criticism, of embracing uncertainty, of accepting ambiguity, of recognising conflicting interests, of encouraging courage and honesty of thought, of seeing mistakes as positive growing points). These are the 'safe conditions' that Nias describes and which she points out allow for – even encourage – 'the statement of alternative viewpoints and the expression of potentially controversial attitudes', which are essential to release the full range of views held in a group so that its members are opened up to alternative explanations and views and thus are enabled 'to alter their own beliefs and attitudes, if they so desire' (Nias 1987, p.11).

Wishing to work at an emancipatory level, Nias points out that individuals should be led to 'question the taken for granted', and understand how it has come about and learn how to change it in the direction of personal emancipation (Nias 1987, p.53). She also makes the points that traditional hierarchies have no place in this process and that group members should not be allowed to become authority dependent as this works against independence of thought.

> The more we are supported in our basic assumptions, especially about ourselves, by the opinions of others whom we respect, love or admire, the less readily will we change them.
> (Nias 1987, p.13)

(She is in fact talking of in-service work here, and it is a matter for debate how far this is appropriate for ITE.)

All the tutors whose work is presented comment on the importance of group work. Robert makes the point in the workshop that he plans in detail for this, giving attention to *how* students will work in groups. Hilma Rask indicates the importance of small group work and role-play. She reports that at the end of the course students commented positively on college-based group work with fellow students. Tom and Robert describe how 'the whole group experienced processes of investigation, mixed grouping, spontaneous and hypothesising talk, deductive reasoning, leadership roles, consensual and co-operative talk and decision-making'. They also tell of how 'student discussion on the use of planning, ... details of group organisation, patterns of work, ... individual's feelings and enthusiasms, revealed insights into the way pupils also learn'. Tutors' high expectations of students play their part here. They also make the point that 'students are expected to reflect on why certain activities were taken and strategies used.'

Strategies and skills

Clearly, getting students to recognise their own values and beliefs and to admit the differences between them are important strategies, as are getting them to explore their own theories and practices and admit uncertainty, explore alternative views and make new connections. This involves drawing them away from calls for technical assistance to the discussion of underlying principles, helping them to see beyond the obvious; helping them to recognise and challenge their present views and values; helping them to use critical reflection-on-action, to recognise theories-in-use under this, and the possible dissonance of these in relation to their espoused theories. In short it means enabling them to theorise about practice.

This in turn means that a range of communication skills − especially conversational or discursive, together with listening and writing skills — are vital. Robert Catt and Tom Sweeney offer us practical examples of their attending in detail to this. They show how they draw attention to body language, the scaffolding language used to support learning and how they point out the relationship between language use and personal and social identity. They also show how a communications model is constructed through student discussion, rather than being imposed, and how it is used by students to conduct an audit of perceived personal communication strengths and weaknesses. And Tom and Robert draw attention to ways in which their drama project developed 'a sophisticated level of personal language skill and intellectual ability'.

Discussion of uncertain problematic issues may mean resisting consensus — as Nias says there is 'a tendency to prefer agreement to disagreement; to avoid open conflict amongst adults' (Nias 1987, p.30). Tom and Robert make the point that in their work early discourse moves quickly to consensus, but indicate that when critical perceptions are sharpened by tutor's questions there is less agreement. They show how they work with an 'awareness of the need to draw in a more representative range of voices' and they point to ways in which their transcripts show the rise of 'oppositional voices . . . in student seminars'. Robert points out that in their own interpretation of this work they call on conversation analysts' highlighting of 'the principles of co-operation and co-ordination'. This certainly means offering students support, being non-threatening, using conversational tone rather than interrogation. Hilma Rask refers to Adler's 'notion of reflection being in a sense an ongoing conversation' and how this fits with the voices that emerge from her own case study. In her study too she tells how a student voiced her dilemma of, on the one hand, wanting to keep to established routines . . . and on the other hand of wanting to allow for the spontaneous moment which she considered to be of vital importance for work with young children. Robert Catt makes the point that his Education Studies sessions are lively and characterised by activities, discussion and presentation. He reports how he and Tom Sweeney 'attempt to make theoretical assumptions explicit . . . aim to provide students with opportunities to discuss theory and, importantly, . . . tease out the values and ideologies with which it is entwined'. Although they are dealing in polemics, their tone is not aggressive. They listen as well as talk.

In fact this work involves all parties in listening as much as talking. The significance of the role of talk in learning is acknowledged in Robert Catt's course by the fact that formal seminars and presentations given by the students to their peers are formally assessed.

And it is clear that succinct and cogent arguments are central to this. Such dialogue, as Brookfield also reminds us, cannot be scripted in advance as it is reciprocal, improvised and involves disagreement, diversity and challenge (see Brookfield 1987, p.238).

Sometimes too, students use writing to clarify their problems. Hilma Rask shows how her student, Elizabeth 'made notes in her [TP] file on possible solutions to present to the team' of adults in her classroom and how she continued to debate in her own written lesson evaluations the advantages and disadvantages of different ways of organising the sessions of classroom work. Hilma makes the point that written evaluations of lessons 'serve as an ongoing dialogue about progress over a range of issues to be shared by the student with teachers and supervisors'. She adds that 'where such evaluations are written with honest critical insight, such records can serve as a source for deeper reflection'. Robert Catt talks of the importance of the observation diary and the school experience journal in encouraging reflective practice. And tutors write for students too. Lynne shows us her writing in a note to her TP student.

This clearly too involves developing the skills of traditional critical thinking, of dialectic, of appreciation, of academic argument, of justification. To achieve this, tutors adopt a facilitator's role, providing resources, raising questions, encouraging students to listen to and to learn from each other and from wider literature, and discreetly shaping the discourse. By this means, in Nias's words, they draw students 'to grapple with the construction of new meanings, for themselves and one another' (Nias 1987, p.52).

Revealing the only clear examples of prudential and moral discourse amongst the five studies, Tom and Robert show how what they call 'reflective discussion stimulated by the drama tended towards broad issues of social justice and the advisability of doing this work with pupils who may have domestic circumstances influenced by a background of criminal activity'. They actually make the point that 'reflection itself introduces moral and ethical issues which present students with professional dilemmas'. It is therefore clear that their work deliberately seeks out and poses such dilemmas in order to stimulate moral discourse. Interestingly, they too were the only tutors who referred to the use of more formal lectures under the particular circumstances of needing to inform students of specific knowledge that they would then use. A further example of concern about moral issues is to be found in Christine Edwards' comments about the National Curriculum and the entitlement of all children to musical education, although her study does not explicitly show her in discussion with students about this.

Brookfield (1987) discusses strategies for facilitating critical thinking (defined in its broadest terms). These include:

- accepting and encouraging diversity and divergence

- resisting artificial resolution of dialectical debate

- being flexible in terms of the format of a discussion

- showing risk-taking and spontaneity

- facilitating and modelling openness and critical analysis

- not seeking for, nor trying to demonstrate, perfection

- showing scepticism of final answers

- recognising that some problems may remain forever a mystery

- sometimes teacher removing him/herself to enable learning to happen

- reflecting back attitudes and valuing speakers.

Challenging ideas is also important. Here, getting the level of the challenge right (so that it is not too aggressive and promotes thinking rather than blanking out) and knowing how, when and where to offer challenge is vital. Lynne challenged her TP student to adopt alternative strategies and between them they challenged the class teacher's ideas. The studies are full of examples of persistent probing and sensitive challenging. And Wade makes the point that this kind of work challenges tutors 'to nurture students' confidence in the worth of their ideas while also encouraging them to reflect on and rethink their views' (Wade 1994, p.240).

Spotting the moment

That tutors do not often draw attention to these aspects of their work is, perhaps, not surprising. (Though it has turned out to be politically disastrous.) The kinds of interaction noted above, can seem like ordinary and everyday activities — and take an experienced eye to recognise them. Further, this apparent ordinariness relates *both* to the points the students make (which tutors spot as providing important opportunities to extend learning) *and* to the skills and strategies of the tutors themselves, which are often so smoothly presented that students do not notice them until perhaps the tutor hands the chair of a discussion over to a student whose performance is less sure. Several tutors refer directly to these issues. Hilma points up the fact that 'incidents emerging [from group discussion] may appear at first glance to be insignificant ... however I hope to illustrate that, when fully attended to, it is these small events which provide deep and lasting consequences for future practice'. She shows how reflection on time management prompted the student to question principles underlying practice and to explore ways of negotiating change. Robert Catt points up Tom Sweeney's skilful support, guidance and direction, his picking up of commonalities, cutting into redundancy and pressing students to clarify and classify and reach deeper understanding implicit in the reported dialogue of their study that at first glance looks very ordinary. He shows how Tom's 'seemingly conversational "scaffolding" structure of the introductory course, and [the] evaluation session' reported on 'has allowed students to make their own way to a pertinent conclusion'. Such student reflection on practice, they would claim, exemplifies the value of 'grounded theory' and the 'importance of socially constructed and conversationally shared awareness'.

The tutors' role

The tutors' role in all of this, then, is to provide the conditions for learning in this way. This includes providing the stimulus (perhaps drawing out critical incidents from shared practice, perhaps using role-play, video, a shared reading as a starting point – certainly starting with the concrete, particular, describable and clearly graspable and moving to the general, the abstract, the more complex). This, no doubt, provides what Wade pinpoints as an important device for success in discussions, namely giving students enough information to feel confident and interested in talking about a topic. Examples from the studies include Christine Edwards' comments that in offering students musical experiences at their own level 'the process will to some extent mirror children's own musical progress and offer valuable insights into the nature of learning in music'. She also refers to debriefing students on a shared lesson where she 'asked them about the elements of pulse and rhythm ... pressed them to trace the development from simple activity to more complex' and stressed the importance of being able to stand back and observe. Wade reports that students see the role of the tutor as crucial to success and failure in discussions (Wade 1994, p.237).

(iii)

Practical discourse

Tutors' and students' achievements

Jackson characterises achievement in teacher development by comparison with what happens when we confront a work of art and are deeply affected by it. He points out that we 'have no clear and unequivocal language for describing that process. As a consequence we revert to metaphor'. He indicates that these metaphors are often based on sight and that 'we speak as though our vision has been altered in some fundamental way', but that in fact what undergoes change is our understanding, not our eyesight (Jackson 1992, p.66). This is also characterised by other familiar metaphors like 'penetrating the mists of our understanding', seeing broader horizons, seeing anew, seeing better than before (see also Nias 1987). Jackson adds the following important point, that as a result of this improved vision:

> we may not *look* like better teachers, at least not to the naked eye. In fact we might even look worse. We might possibly develop a more hesitant manner ... We also may not *feel* any better as a teacher either. Again, we might actually feel worse, at least temporarily: more doubt-ridden, puzzled, sadder perhaps. After all, sadness and wisdom are not incompatible ...
> (Jackson 1992, p.67)

This certainly warns us against looking for simplistic signs of achievement in teacher education. Further, the long-term nature of education (in that much of what is learnt does not cash out into immediate visible achievements) together with the nature of teaching (in that it is an open capacity and can never be mastered) mean that ITE tutors inevitably cannot hope to see most of the real achievements of the fully fledged professional teacher that they have worked towards. There are, of course, the statements of 'positive feedback' at the end of teaching practices, but on the whole the kinds of achievements that tutors see and value are those which are part of the processes of learning. In this, too, then, tutors have to develop an ability to recognise students' achievements for what they are during the course and to work further upon them. This is often done quietly and behind the scenes. It is hardly surprising, therefore, that students themselves are often unaware of the tutor's role in this and that the public have been easily persuaded that tutors make no contribution to teacher preparation.

In these studies, tutors have, in fact, commented on students' achievements in learning through the work described, under the following main categories: increased professionalism; finding a voice; growing awareness; increased insight; gaining understanding; developing critical *dispositions* (although they mostly do not aspire to the emancipatory); and becoming reflective. For example, Hilma points to the increased professionalism of her two nursery students which is revealed in their greater sensitivity to the problems of managing adults, as shown in their interview at the end of their course. Tom refers to the emergence of professional voices during his work. Robert points to the achievements of Sylvia who, in a supportive environment, is able to speak openly about what could be a damaging criticism from a pupil. Hilma speaks of a student who 'had begun to find her voice, [and] grapple with the complex nature of collaborative team work', and tells of the voices in which both students 'gave powerful testimony to just how far they had travelled over the final two years of the course'.

It is in the growth of awareness, insight and understanding, however, that the main achievements have occurred. The growth of awareness, of course, might be visible at a practical level, as in Tom's case, where he refers to his students' growing awareness of their own ability to manage a class. Or it might be a growing intellectual awareness (sometimes visible only to tutors, sometimes penetrating students' consciousness). For example, Hilma identifies her students' growing awareness of the nature of collaborative teaching, the greater awareness of students at the end of the course about the complexities of teaching, and how a student battled towards a practical solution and became aware of the need to listen to others. She also talks of one student who became more self-aware by starting to look critically at herself and her own attitudes as a team member. And Tom's drama evaluation begins with a student comment about what the group had achieved.

In terms of insight, again tutors report a range of achievements. Gaining insight, as in all learning, is a patchy affair. Tom reports Mark's insight, that all the students had been actively involved in the group work (which for him was a new thought), but at the same time indicates his lack of self-awareness as a group member. He also talks about students having gained more insight into drama itself. Hilma shows a student recognising an insight about practice in the reported view: 'Sometimes a child just needed someone else.' She also shows how Elizabeth came to see that each team member had developed an acute awareness of when to intervene in situations in the nursery. Christine identifies her students gaining a 'brief insight into the delicate role of the teacher as facilitator and encourager in creative work in the arts' and the 'fine line between imposing ideas and helping a group who are struggling'. (She does not, however, at this point engage with students about the nature of professional judgement and the questions of procedural, prudential and moral nature.) The students Hilma interviewed at the end of the course responded to her questions 'with impressive sensitivity' and demonstrated insights into the strategies of managing a team which they need even in their first teaching appointment. She offers in evidence the students' words: 'I think you've really got to get alongside them . . . value where they are coming from and what good practices they have got.' And one insight leads to another as Hilma ponders on the applicability of this to her own work with students.

Tutors claim improved understanding on the part of students too. But, again, this is in relationship to the students' remarkable lack of knowledge about teaching at the beginning of the course and might well be overlooked by an experienced teacher who might expect such understanding as a base. For example, Hilma reports that Elizabeth had begun to understand that the role of nursery teacher was more complex and varied than she had at first realised. And Robert reports that 'theoretical connections are [made] out of an understanding of practice'.

Alongside this, too, there is evidence of some development of critical thinking and of the beginnings of self-criticism that will take students into a more independent mode. Robert speaks of introducing students to 'that critical disposition of mind which will enable them to both cope with and move beyond immediate professional concerns'. And the study itself gives evidence of the achievement of this. Christine shows how students were able to deduce from the way pupils worked in groups that their teacher involved them regularly in creative collaborative learning. She also talks about the collaborative nature of the students' course and the way that they support each other and share ideas − about how students learn from their mistakes and grow into self-criticism and reflection. Hilma speaks of how students begin to value constructive criticism, and shows how they come to make important distinctions between outsiders and insiders in the nursery.

Students are also shown in the studies as having developed reflective habits of mind. Marking the beginning of reflective thinking, Robert remarks of David's written work: 'of significance ... is the shift of mood away from the earlier shared hilarity ... resulting from some obvious reflective attention'. This is a highly significant incident, showing as it does the value for David, *first* of time spent in a sheltered environment where he can utter, share and refine his first meaning-making about the challenge he received from a pupil, and *second* of time spent maturing this understanding in written work that also needed time and space away from the action. It is not an accident of history that both these spoken and written activities in ITE have traditionally happened not in the schools where the action is, but in the reflective calm of the university.

Robert also claims, with Tom, that: 'there is an emergence of what Schön characterises as "reflection-on-action". That is, student teachers are encouraged to reflect on events from their own teaching and to generate questions, possibilities and insights from their practice as they are involved in it' – and we see examples of this in the study. Hilma comments on the way a student 'had begun to reflect even more deeply on her underlying beliefs about ways in which children learn and how a team of adults can facilitate this in the nursery'. She also makes the point that both students highlighted the importance of the development of personal theories through the taught course and how important it was to be aware of underpinning principles of practice in the early years. Tom, in his drama project, reporting on the student who tried out the ideas in his own TP, comments that the student's 'ability to react to unplanned events, to reflect-in-action, was evidenced in the student's response to pupils' questions'.

These, then, are examples of the achievements of this aspect of ITE, and it remains to stress some of the conditions necessary for this kind of work.

(iv)

Conditions necessary for critical enquiry

We have seen that in preparation for successful practice and membership of their profession, student teachers need to be offered education that is, in Oakeshott's terms, 'an engagement rather than an heirloom' (Oakeshott 1972, p.23). And it is surely clear that the engagement in which we need to involve them is that of critical enquiry – of which both practical discourse and reflective writing are a part, as is also the investigation of practice itself.

A tradition of critical enquiry should arguably be both central to a healthy teaching profession and be the basis of university learning (see Pring 1994). Indeed, it seems incontestable that the meaning-making associated with understanding practice in schools should be located in the university. McLaughlin, for example, makes the point that 'there is an important difference between the sort of critical reflection which takes place in a university seminar, where students can discuss matters in the abstract, and that which takes place in the context of a particular school' (McLaughlin 1994, p.159). And it would seem reasonable to claim that the studies presented above give credence to this.

The university, then, provides the detachment that Oakeshott argues is a vital component of the conditions for education. He describes the school (but this would arguably apply equally to the School of Education – though *not* for obvious reasons the 'training school') as 'detachment from the immediate, local world of the learner, its current concerns and the directions it gives to his attention'. He continues (in terms which still apply thirty years after he wrote them – and which apply strikingly to the education of the student teacher) by pointing out that school:

> is a place apart in which the heir may encounter his moral and intellectual inheritance, not in terms in which it is being used in the current engagements and occupations of the world outside (where much of it is forgotten, neglected, obscured, vulgarized or abridged, and where it appears only in scraps as investments in immediate enterprises) but as an estate, entire, unqualified and unencumbered. 'School' is an emancipation achieved in a continuous redirection of attention.
>
> (Oakeshott 1972, pp.24–5)

Thus, just as engagement in practical activities for the student teacher demands (in Schön's terms) a sheltered practicum in which to experiment, try out activities, be safe to engage in extending practices and take the necessary risks which we know are involved in learning, so critical enquiry demands a proper place – a safe 'praxicum' perhaps – in which to engage in activities proper to education. And Oakeshott's words still apply here too:

Here, the learner is animated, not by the inclinations he brings with him, but by intimations of excellences and aspirations he has never yet dreamed of; here he may encounter, not answers to 'loaded' questions of 'life', but questions which have never before occurred to him; here he may acquire new 'interests' and pursue them uncorrupted by the need for immediate results; here he may learn to seek satisfactions he had never yet imagined or wished for.
(Oakeshott 1972, p.25)

In the university, then, there is (or should be) the expertise, the library resources and the time and space to enable student teachers to see their practice in a new light. These are the conditions in which their theorising about practice (as described in the studies) needs to be nurtured. And these matters lie behind the work described in Part 2, although they are not immediately visible. And others too have pointed in these directions.

Rudduck usefully summarises the expertise needed in tutors as an analytic perspective, fed by observation across a range of settings and sharpened by research knowledge. This, she argues, enables HE tutors to understand the problems and achievements of teachers and learners in a range of contexts, 'taking into account social, historical and ideological perspectives', being well informed about structures and practices in schools, and understanding and knowing how to help others to understand the pressures and values that influence such structures and practices (see Rudduck 1992, p.160).

Osterman and Kottkamp usefully analyse some conditions for nurturing reflection. These include matters that can be *deduced* from the studies − like the need for an environment characterised by openness and trust and a supportive group setting where discussion of a problem is not interpreted as admission of failure and where information disclosed will not be used against the discloser. Such a situation also needs a facilitator who 'assumes responsibility for ensuring the participants' safety' (Osterman and Kottkamp 1993, pp.43−6). Further perusal of the studies would provide further characteristics. More work needs to be carried out in demonstrating and explaining to the public such educational engagements and their necessary conditions.

Given the vital importance of the tutors' role in HE, and the effort that has been put into understanding and refining their practice inside the HEIs, it is amazing that more studies of this kind have not been forthcoming in the public domain. The following chapter makes some suggestions about how such work might both be encouraged and used by the partners.

194

References

Abercrombie, M.J.L. and Terry, P.M. (1978) *Talking to learn: improving teaching and learning in small groups*. Guildford: SRHE.

Adler, S. (1991) 'The reflective practitioner and the curriculum of teacher education', *Journal of Education for Teaching*, 17 (2), pp.139–50.

Bligh, D. (1986) *Teach thinking by discussion*. Guildford: SRHE/NFER/Nelson

Bridges, D., Elliott, J. and Klass, C. (1986) 'Performance appraisal as naturalistic enquiry: a report of the fourth Cambridge Conference on educational evaluation', *Cambridge Journal of Education*, 16 (3), pp.221–33.

Brookfield, S. D. (1987) *Developing critical thinkers: challenging adults to explore alternative ways of thinking and acting*. Milton Keynes: Open University Press.

Carr, D. (1993) 'Questions of competence', *British Journal of Educational Studies*, 41 (3), pp.253–72.

Costa, A. (1990) 'Teacher behaviours that promote discussion', Wilen, W.W. (Ed.) (1990) *Teaching and learning through discussion: the theory, research and practice of the discussion method*. Springfield Illinois: Charles C. Thomas, pp.45–78.

Fish, D. (1995) *Quality mentoring for student teachers: a principled approach to practice*. London: David Fulton.

Gitlin, A. (1990) 'Educative research, voice and school change', *Harvard Educational Review*, 60 (3), pp.443–66. (Cited in Johnson (1994).)

Grundy, S. (1987) *Curriculum: product or praxis*. London: Falmer Press.

Jackson, P.W. (1992) 'Helping teachers develop', in Hargreaves, A. and Fullan, M. (Eds) (1992) *Understanding teacher development*. London: Cassell, pp.62–74.

James, M. (1989) 'Negotiation and dialogue in student assessment and appraisal', in Simons, H. and Elliott, J. (Eds) (1989) *Rethinking appraisal and assessment*. Milton Keynes: Open University Press, pp.149–60.

Johnston, S. (1994) 'Conversations with student teachers – enhancing the dialogue of learning to teach', *Teaching and Teacher Education*, 10 (1), pp.71–82.

McLaughlin, T.H. (1994) 'Mentoring and the demands of reflection', in Wilkin, M. and Sankey, D. (Eds) (1994) *Collaboration and transition in initial teacher training*. London: Kogan Page, pp.151–60.

Nias, J. (1987) *Seeing anew: teachers' theories of action*. Geelong: Deakin University.

Oakeshott, M. (1972) 'Education: the engagement and its frustration', in Dearden, R.F., Hirst, P.H. and Peters, R.S. (Eds) (1972) *Education and the development of reason*. London: Routledge and Kegan Paul, pp.19–49.

Osterman, K. and Kottkamp, R. (1993) *Reflective practice for educators: improving schooling through professional development*. California: Corwin Press Inc.

Pring, R. (1994) 'The year 2000', in Wilkin, M. and Sankey, D. (Eds) (1994) *Collaboration and transition in initial teacher training*. London: Kogan Page, pp.174–89.

Reid, W. (1979) *Thinking about the curriculum: the nature and treatment of curriculum problems.* London: Routledge and Kegan Paul.

Rudduck, J. (1978) *Learning through small group discussion: a study of seminar work in higher education.* Guildford: SRHE.

Rudduck, J. (1992) 'Practitioner research and programs of initial teacher education', in Russell, T. and Munby, H. (Eds) (1992) *Teachers and teaching: from classroom to reflection.* London: Falmer Press, pp.156–70.

Wade, R. (1994) 'Teacher education students' views on class discussion: implications for fostering critical reflection', *Teaching and Teacher Education,* **10** (2), pp.231–43.

Zeichner, K. (1987) 'Preparing reflective teachers: an overview of instructional strategies which have been employed in preservice teacher education', *International Journal of Educational Research,* **11**, pp.565–75.

CHAPTER 10

Quality Education for Student Teachers: Clarifying the Tutor's Role

Introduction

The government has provided, in *Circulars* *9/92* and *14/93,* the required legal framework for both secondary and primary ITE for at least the 1990s. The Education Act 1994 has opened the way to, but not yet required absolutely, school-centred ITT. The Open University is already extensively embarked on a distance-learning approach to ITT. But writers are already arguing that ITE without an HE contribution will not be able to be sustained throughout the 1990s (see, for example, Pring 1994, p.182). And whatever the overall structure of the 'reformed' system, still a considerable number of decisions will have to be made 'on the ground'. First there is the decision about the overall model to opt for (distance-learning, school-based or school-centred), and second there are decisions to be made about how to operate each specific version of a course within both the government requirements and the assumptions implicit in the overall model chosen.

It is in these decisions that teachers and tutors still have some power to negotiate the future. And it is these decisions that are problematic. In order to respond rationally to this, the providers of ITE need to address those problems they can make some impact on, and try to find rational ways forward from where we are. Although the kinds of activities described in the above studies are not necessarily directly generalisable, and it is neither permissible nor reasonable to claim that current tutors all operate in the ways described above, the studies might nevertheless offer future providers of ITE fuel for debate about the content and processes that ought to be part of preparing future teachers. It is hoped, too, that it might also provoke other HE staff to offer the public arena further evidence about tutors' work, which will extend the knowledge-base of the debate.

(i)

Addressing the problems

First, then, decisions need to be made about the overall shape of ITE courses, and the central issue here is the role in them of HE. Then attention needs to be paid afresh to the curriculum for ITE, and decisions need to be made about the goals, intentions, content and processes to be deployed.

The future role of HE in teacher preparation

A number of writers, so far mainly from the older established universities (Alexander 1990; Barber 1993; Golby (in Schnur and Golby 1995); Kelly 1993; Pring 1994) are now setting out views about the importance of retaining an HE dimension in future ITE. Pring, for example, argues for 'flourishing departments of educational studies, with a distinctive agenda worthy of universities and closely involved in the training of teachers' (Pring 1994, p.181). He suggests that school-based ITT will inevitably run into difficulties because it has been so badly set up and believes that the future of universities in ITE should be assured because 'teachers themselves see how closely connected are their own aspirations to professional status with a university partnership in which distinctive roles of each partner are clearly recognized and respected' (Pring 1994, p.182). (I shall argue later that such 'distinctiveness' should not also mean 'different' in the way the current circulars suggest.) But I would want to add here that the inevitability of HEIs' future involvement in ITE ought also to be because (however belatedly) tutors themselves, teachers and the public recognise the significance, importance and distinctive nature of their educational contribution to ITE (including the kind portrayed in this book as well as grander and more visible ones seen in some older universities).

Pring continues by recognising that the validity of university-based knowledge has in the past been dislocated from practice and that lecturers too often remained as strangers to practices about which they theorised. (I have argued elsewhere that such descriptions fitted some university departments better than those of the colleges (Fish 1989 and 1995). Pring then claims that it is the role of the university to provide:

> first, a centre of expertise relevant to teaching; second, a critical tradition within which both the trainee and the experienced teacher might learn in an informed and questioning way to examine educational practice; and, third, a centre of relevant research. In the absence of these three 'services' − the distinctive jobs of a university − it is difficult to see how teaching can long maintain its claim to be a profession, a claim that must be based upon an expertise grounded in specialist knowledge, in critical enquiry and in relevant research.
> (Pring 1994, p.187)

Barber offers similar arguments, saying that 'higher education can be the link to the ferment of ideas and argument about what makes good teachers and good education' (Barber 1993, p.258). Schnur and Golby go further, arguing that 'education must present a vision of the future as well as one for coping with the present' and that it is the responsibility of teacher educators to, 'see that future teachers are at least aware of alternative views and historic endeavors in schooling' (Schnur and Golby 1995, in press). They also say that the university traditionally has captured, examined, researched and developed these matters, in an independent way. The university, they argue, should develop research into teaching and effectively disseminate its research findings:

> [There will be a] need to focus scholarly productivity on the improvement of practice ... [Staff] will be interlocutors between theory and practice.
> (Schnur and Golby 1995, in press)

They see school-based ITE as offering creative opportunities in that direction because 'professional knowledge is generated in the professional school of the university in close conjunction with the practising profession and its clients'. What such a school could produce is 'a set of studies that deals with practice on its own terms, regarding the arts of teaching not as the application of knowledge derived from elsewhere but as created in situ'. They conclude with a set of recommendations for viable 'schools or colleges of education' (see Schnur and Golby 1995, in press).

Pring also argues that future success lies in joint enterprise, a comment which seems to echo the uncomfortably prophetic comment: 'If we do not go forward together we may not go forward at all' (Fish 1989, p.198).

The university response to government manipulation, then, is beginning in earnest. It is, however, not entirely a healthy matter that its proponents in the early stages at least, have come *only* from the rarefied air of older universities and those who have the wider vision of senior staff. By virtue of their reputation and position, they are disconnected from the daily cut and thrust of ITE in practice. We need more, much more, from those with a more lowly, but a more immediate involvement. But then, of course, both government and their own establishments keep them too busy to raise their pens let alone their heads. However, it is they who in the end will probably take a lead in creating the new curriculum for school-based ITE.

The future curriculum for teacher preparation

Given the new circulars, courses throughout the nineties will probably be being revised and designed all the time, and all tutors and teachers joining courses already designed will need to contribute to the discussions about shaping the practical aspects of their operation. What have to be faced by the partners then are classic curriculum problems. The procedures for addressing them ought therefore to be those of practical discourse (in which tutors should be expert), and the parties to that discourse clearly ought to be representatives of the schools and the HEI, the teachers immediately involved and the education tutors. This is in accord with government requirements for school-based ITE. A principled base for negotiation ought to be established at the start but also will need to be refined as the deliberations proceed. The key questions to be deliberated ought to be the basic philosophy for the course, and the course design issues including the intentions, the principles of procedure, the resources available and the present starting points — which will have to include competences and quality control, but need not focus upon them exclusively (see Fish 1995, for a detailed consideration of these matters).

Arguably for any *educational* version of teacher preparation, the procedures of deliberation about the course ought to involve recognising the procedural, prudential and moral questions underlying the apparently simple practical ones. There ought to be a clear recognition of the present contributions of tutors as well as teachers to ITE and the need for education as well as training within the course. In short, the illuminations about the tutors' roles offered above ought to be taken into account in the new arrangements, though how such contributions will be offered, by whom, when and where will be able to be answered only within specific instances of a course.

Thus what has been presented in Chapters 3 to 8 of this book ought to offer some illumination to the debates to be held. The following three issues indicate ways in which the level of the debate between the partners about ITE might be raised.

A consideration of goals

It is always important to be clear about the goals of an enterprise, and this is bound to be an area for deliberation. The goal suggested by the work reported in this book is that of preparation of a reflective practitioner for a profession rather than a technician for classroom delivery of the National Curriculum. The partners will need to be sure what they are seeking to achieve in this respect and then how they will seek to achieve it. For example, what exactly will be the role, in a course with these wider goals, of work in a school classroom? How will the partners ensure that it relates to wider understandings about schools and other classrooms? How will the work of an individual school relate to the broader traditions of education and the issues discussed above of justice, equity, morality and ethics? How will the uncertain nature of practical decisions (about aims, teaching and learning, assessment, organisation and management and the wider social and political context of professional activity) be brought to students' attention and how will they be engaged in practical discourse about them?

Some important distinctions

The work of Alexander helps delineate some important distinctions that need to be recognised at the start of deliberations. He points to the sharp distinction to be made between the enabling level of work in ITE (that is the administrative aspects of the partners' role) and the educational aspects. He also indicates the need to consider the role of college and school as distinct from the roles of tutor and teacher. (And in secondary schools it is important to be clear whether responsibilities are those of the whole school, the department or an individual teacher.) He makes the point that it is important to clarify sharply:

1. the kinds of skills and knowledge that each partner can offer the student. (This may be very different in different partnerships.) For example, there will be some teachers who can function in the ways we have shown tutors operating

2. the ways that each partner views and values the student

3. the expectations and responsibilities that the partners will have in terms of quality control issues.

Alexander also notes the importance of different institutions exchanging information about procedures and arrangements, about good practice, about how ITE is seen, about each other's practical situations. In this respect there are also useful requirements made within the two main circulars and their Catenotes.

The roles of school and college

It is also important to establish a clear set of principles from the start of deliberations about what school-based work for students can provide and what college-based work should offer. Enough has already been said about the possibilities of college-based work. Clearly school-based work is practical work, focussed on the specific, the idiosyncratic and involves great expertise of teachers (some of which is so deeply embedded in their practice that it is invisible). But it does not always relate to the visions of practice that students bring with them to the course, is not always of generalisable value, and it is not always clear to students why they should pay attention to it. It is also difficult for them to gain access to teachers' greatest expertise in some cases. As Stones points out, learning on the job is restricted to teachers' experience, and it is not systematic.

> It is therefore limited in its general accessibility. Teachers are, thus, doubly constrained by the view of teaching as a craft in which the main function of practitioners is passing on information. On the one hand, current practitioners' skills and knowledge are confined to their own experience and, therefore, limited. On the other hand, the lack of underlying theory confines any discussion between experienced and beginning teachers to surface activities of teaching.
> (Stones 1992, p.9)

And Kelly also offers food for thought in these matters in respect of the teacher's role in ITE.

> Practical advice is fine; but it is of little value and may, indeed, be positively dangerous if it is not accompanied by guidance on how to hold it up to the kind of constant challenge and critique which ... is the essence of any form of academic study in a university setting.
> (Kelly 1993, p.133)

These points are useful if only to remind us that the roles, contributions and responsibilities of all partners will need to be carefully considered. Perspectives on the kinds of responsibilities likely to devolve upon teachers as mentors can be found in Fish (1995).

Ways of exploiting present strengths
There surely can be little doubt in the light of all that has been said that both schools and colleges, teachers and tutors can and should contribute to the preparation of the student teacher. Both can provide opportunities for considering the particular and the general. Both can offer initiation into practical discourse, albeit from differing points of view and differing experiences and practices. This means not only that all the strengths of both partners need to be harnessed to the task, but, crucially, that both partners, as David Carr points out, are contributing their different expertise *to the same overall task*. This is in contradiction to the view in the circulars, which is derived from what Carr argues is a mistaken belief, that it is possible to atomise teaching into a number of competences and that different partners can attend to providing students with different skills. He helpfully argues that both partners' work ought to be about how to 'exploit professional wisdom and insight to good or best effect'. As a result, he argues:

> From this perspectice teacher educators have a professional obligation to address serious questions about the proper balance of academic studies and opportunities for practical experience ... [and] observe a certain proper traditional division of labour between college tutors and school based trainers with respect to professional preparation; to recognise that, as well as receiving proper help and guidance from seasoned practitioners in schools, prospective teachers also require to be exposed to academically rigorous, informed and up-to-date tuition from scholars who are at the leading edge of serious enquiry into conceptual and empirical problems about education.
> (Carr, D. 1993, p.269)

He also makes the important point that teachers' professional competence ought to be judged in terms of their understanding and professional judgement rather than simply their skills as observed. This would suggest that the partners might well wish to consider some means of assessment beyond the basic competences required by government (see Fish 1995, Chapter 7).

A final proposal

In order to create a successful new 'reformed' system of ITE, there is much to be done to investigate, reflect upon and improve the practice of the partners in teacher preparation; there is much about which partners in serious deliberations with each other might (given time) be able to be creative; and there is help and encouragement at hand – including the work reported above. But with new regulations and new Acts following each other fast, there is no time to treat these matters properly. The government has already recognised a similar situation with regard to the reforms of the National Curriculum. There it has seen fit to accept the Dearing recommendation of a five-year moratorium on further change. This publication proposes that government makes a similar move to put further change in ITE on hold so that HE staff can consider the roots of their practices (in a wide variety of ways including those shown by the writers of these studies) and establish clear rationales and agreed frameworks that will set the partnership that is necessary to ITE on a proper footing. This is a serious matter and should be given due time. After all, if the partners fail to work together and ITE becomes school-centred ITT, the future may see the production of trained teachers who are skilled in observable competences but who are not able to educate our children.

References

Alexander, R. (1990) 'Partnership in initial teacher training: confronting the issues', in Booth, M., Furlong, J. and Wilkin, M. (Eds) (1990) *Partnership in initial teacher training*. London: Cassell, pp.59–73.

Barber, M. (1993) 'The truth about partnership', *Journal of Education for Teaching*, 19 (3), pp.255–62.

Carr, D. (1993) 'Questions of competence', *British Journal of Educational Studies*, 41 (3), pp.253–72.

Fish, D. (1989) *Learning through practice in initial teacher training: a challenge for the partners*. London: Kogan Page.

Fish, D. (1995) *Quality mentoring for student teachers: a principled approach to practice*. London: David Fulton.

Kelly, A.V. (1993) 'Education as a field of study in a university: challenge, critique, dialogue, debate', *Journal of Education for Teaching*, 19 (2), pp.125–39.

Pring, R. (1994) 'The year 2000', in Wilkin, M. and Sankey, D. (Eds) (1994) *Collaboration and Transition in initial teacher training*. London: Kogan Page, pp.174–89.

Schnur, J. and Golby, M. (1995, in press) 'Teacher education: a university mission?', *Journal of Teacher Education*, 46 (1).

Stones, E. (1992) *Quality teaching: a sample of cases*. London: Routledge.

Index